FREEDOM OF ANGELS

BERNADETTE FAHY

Now working as a counsellor in private practice in
Dublin, Bernadette trained in Counselling Psychology
at the University of East London, where she obtained a
first class honours degree. She gained an M.Sc in Counselling Psychology from Roehampton Institute-Surrey
University. She spent almost ten years of her childhood
in Goldenbridge orphanage from age seven to sixteen.
She writes on institutional abuse for various newspapers
and also speaks at conferences on the topic.

FREEDOM OF ANGELS

BERNADETTE FAHY

THE O'BRIEN PRESS
DUBLIN

First published 1999 by The O'Brien Press Ltd.,
20 Victoria Road, Dublin 6, Ireland
Tel. +353 1 4923333; Fax. +353 1 4922777
email: books@obrien.ie
website: http://www.obrien.ie
Reprinted 1999

ISBN: 0-86278-595-2

British Library Cataloguing-in-publication Data
Fahy, Bernadette
Freedom of angels : surviving Goldenbridge Orphanage
1.Fahy, Bernadette 2.Goldenbridge Orphanage
3.Orphans - Ireland - Dublin - Biography
4.Orphanages - Ireland - Dublin - History
I.Title
941.8'35'082

    2 3 4 5 6 7 8 9 10
99 00 01 02 03 04 05 06 07

The O'Brien Press receives
assistance from

The Arts Council
An Chomhairle Ealaíon

Layout and design: The O'Brien Press Ltd.
Cover photograph: the author age 6, with aunt. Author's own.
Printing: Cox & Wyman Ltd.

ACKNOWLEDGEMENTS

Over the many years that I have been researching the subject of institutional abuse, many individuals gave generously of their time and personal recollections. It was often extremely painful for them to re-open old wounds which some thought were long since hidden or buried. Their honesty and courage in opening their hearts and minds to me about the horrific stories of their childhood spent in institutional care I trust and hope was ultimately a healing experience for them. To them I give my sincere and personal gratitude for the privilege of allowing me to share their experiences.

To my brothers Christopher, Michael and their families I say a special thank you for their support, especially to Christopher who patiently tutored me in the art of computing. To my extended family of supportive relatives I also say thank you. I also want to thank my neighbours Peg, John and Frances who kindly fed and nurtured me throughout this project.

A heartfelt appreciation is given to P.J.Cantwell, manager, and Sylvia Graham, assistant manager, at TSB bank, Inchicore, for their encouragement and support without which this project could not have materialised. I wish also to acknowledge the healing power of those many people who helped sustain me and the thousands of other people who were raised in institutions all over Ireland and elsewhere. I want them to know that the love they imparted was a source of inspiration to us and went a considerable way towards healing the hurt of our early lives. This book would not have been written without the commitment of my publisher Michael O'Brien. I very much value the practical support, advice, time, patience and reassurance that Íde ní Laoghaire, my editor, gave throughout the writing of my story. To all the staff at O'Brien Press who were always cheerful, courteous and helpful to me, I say a big thank you.

Last but not least I wish to thank Carmel McDonnell Byrne for her administrative skills and file retrieval systems. A special acknowledgement is offered to my four-legged angel Jefra, my faithful dog, who sat patiently at my feet throughout the writing of this book.

DEDICATION

To each and every person who endured any or all
of their precious years of childhood in the institutional care
of the State or of religious orders in Ireland
and throughout the world

– CONTENTS –

BOOK ONE: *My Life in the Orphanage*

1   Early Memories *page* 11
2   Mornings in Hell 22
3   The Monkey and the Beads 40
4   Days of Judgement 50
5   Playtime Horrors 66
6   Holy Terrors 76
7   All Things Bright and Beautiful 91
8   Growing Pains 107
9   Last Years 128
10 Why the Cruelty? 135

BOOK TWO: *The Healing Process –
Recovering from the Experience*

11 Stigmatised! 153
12 Attitudes to Sexuality 162
13 Living with Families Again 169
14 A Half-way Home 175
15 Addictive Tendencies 184
16 Independence 187
17 Escape Route – Emigration 193
18 Patterns of Disintegration 196
19 Who Am I, After All? 205
20 A Personal Journey 210

– BOOK ONE –

MY LIFE IN THE ORPHANAGE

CHAPTER ONE

– Early Memories –

I entered Goldenbridge orphanage in my communion outfit. My mother dressed me that morning as usual. I remember wearing my black patent leather shoes and white socks. My mother had knitted the socks herself – beautiful socks they were, plain at the foot, with a fancy pattern up to the top. I still remember how comfortable they were, and how white. And my first communion coat. It was a beautiful coat – light beige with dark stripes going down it and across it, and a lovely fur collar. My mother dressed my twin brother, Michael, in his communion suit. I don't remember what my other brother, just a year younger than us, had on him, but no doubt he was suitably attired for the occasion. My youngest brother, Christopher, who was just 16 months old, was dressed in a red and white one-piece outfit that made him look like a little Santa. Thus we were delivered to the orphanage at Goldenbridge.

We spent the previous night at the house of a friend of my father's. Rather, some of the family did. I spent the night in my father's taxi. I remember the leather of the seats – beautifully stitched, brown leather. The car was very comfortable. I can see my father in the driver's seat, just looking out through the windscreen. It was a dark night, and he continued to look straight ahead. I concentrated on the back of his head. He didn't utter a word to me or my twin brother. It's as if we weren't there. I like to think that he was reflecting on the family situation and wondering what to do about it. We children didn't speak to each other either. Silence reigned. In my head, however, I was very conscious that I was badly in need of a toilet. I held on to this feeling for what seemed like a very long time. Perhaps I thought it was too late to disturb the household. Whatever the reason, I didn't feel it was okay to tell my father. I sensed that something was seriously amiss. Then all went blank.

My twin, Michael, recollects that next morning, after preparing us, our mother and father took the four of us to the Dublin Health Authority in Lord Edward Street, in the heart of Dublin. There we waited for hours with my parents. Then we all got into my father's car to go to the orphanage. We children had no idea where we were going, but we were soon to find out.

We were taken to a place full of large, grey buildings. As I remember it now, the orphanage stood behind the convent, hidden from view as you went down the driveway. It was a tall, austere, grey building contrasting sharply with the convent building, which was more pleasing to the eye and faced the wide avenue. It was enormous, so big that the tallest adults looked tiny against the huge grey backdrop. The lowest windows were so high off the ground that visitors could not see through them. Whatever the place looked like to adults to us small children it looked menacing and threatening.

It was the afternoon of a summer's day, 5 June 1961, just four days before my seventh birthday, when we turned in at the gates of Goldenbridge, passed the sign which proclaimed it as an establishment of the Sisters of Mercy, and drove along the wide avenue to the orphanage. A nun met us at the front door. She took our coats and put them away. They were stored in a small room with racks on the walls, racks too high for us children to reach. The interior of this room was revealed to us only when new children came and had their coats stored in the same ritualistic way. These coats now belonged in another, lost world, that world we had just come from, a world that was no longer ours, though we did not yet know it. We belonged to the Sisters of Mercy now.

That is where my memories of Goldenbridge begin. A woman took us by the hand and led us along a corridor. She was gentle at the time and I wasn't frightened of her. She took us to a yard which was full of children. It was an eerie scene. For one thing, the children were quiet. There was none of the dashing about, the chattering and the screeching you would expect to find. At one wall was a big door with three steps leading up to it. On the steps were what looked like hundreds of shoes, all lined up in pairs. Two girls sat on the steps polishing the shoes. The other children stood around in their socks, waiting.

The woman put us on swings. Then she went away. I noticed another odd thing: there were all those children in the yard, yet the swings were empty. There was an enormous roundabout in the middle of the yard. That too, stood empty. I sat motionless on the swing, looking about me at the silent children and at the girls polishing the shoes. I had absolutely no idea what I was doing there.

Suddenly we were all in a big recreation hall, which we later came to know as the Rec. The room itself was enormous with a hard wooden bench around three of its sides and a stage at the top. The ceiling was striking in that there were narrow bars right across it, and I used to wonder if they were used for hanging people in the old days. The Rec was the largest room in Goldenbridge and it was intended as a playroom for us hundreds of children when it rained outside, as it often did. I was to come to know this room very well indeed. It would be the setting for some of the worst scenes of terror I would see in Goldenbridge.

You could say that the immediate cause of our incarceration in Goldenbridge was that our aunt and uncle couldn't keep us at their house anymore. We had been living there, my mother and my brothers, after our father had walked out on us yet again. He had left us, a few weeks earlier, to return to his other family, his real wife and the children of their marriage. My brothers and I didn't know anything about all of this; we thought we were his family. My father was one of those men who had two families; the others were the legitimate family. My mother knew about it, and spoke about it on rare occasions after we left Goldenbridge. My father simply walked away from his responsibility for us. Walking out on us meant walking out on his obligation to pay the rent on our home in Ranelagh. That's how we ended up in my aunt's house, a house which already had plenty of children to be catered for. Soon it all became too much for her, and we had to go.

We could say that my father's desertion of us was the real cause of what happened. Or we could blame my mother, society, the Church, the State or whomsoever you wish – to us children it was all the same who was blamed. But it is nevertheless important to understand this: the maltreatment of the children who lived in Goldenbridge did not begin with the Sisters of Mercy. A significant number of us had been rejected before we ever arrived there. Some parents, such as my mother, wanted to keep us but the powers that be, whether Church or State, did not deem this possible, nor did they attempt to make it possible with financial or other support systems. Ironically, soon after we arrived in Goldenbridge, my mother was offered and took a job, rearing the children of a wealthy business family in Dublin. She continued this throughout the duration of our time in Goldenbridge and I felt angry and upset about that. It seemed she was perfectly capable of rearing a family when financial resources were available to her. Such was the fate of families who were not privileged to be wealthy, and the state did nothing to help them.

Meanwhile I went to bed in the Sacred Heart dormitory on that first night. It was a very long room with rows of beds in straight lines. I lay there, worrying about my brothers. Where were they sleeping? I didn't know. And where was the baby, my 16-month-old brother, Christopher? I had not seen them since the woman had put us on the swings. Nobody had told me anything about them. I soon came to learn that the Sacred Heart was known as the 'wet-the-bed' dormitory, probably because younger children slept there and, I might safely assume, were likely to be anxious and nervous and therefore more prone than the bigger girls to wetting their beds.

That first night, and for some months afterwards, I slept near the top of the dormitory. Although the bed was old and springy, the mattress had a lovely big hole in the middle. I fitted into it snugly and it fast became my place of refuge in those early days. But there were some hurdles to get through first. When we went to bed we were all ordered to lie with our heads facing the wall. This was to make sure that we didn't talk to each other, and went to sleep as quickly as possible. The staff, once we were asleep, were free for some hours, so they were highly motivated to induce us to sleep, fast.

They played tricks on us. One that I clearly recall was a staff member telling us that the first child asleep would get a sweet put under her pillow. Then she would say out loud, 'X is asleep first, so I'm going to put a sweet under her pillow.' She would come down and punch us to test if we really were asleep. We, with eyes firmly closed, would pretend to be asleep and she would go through the motions of putting an imaginary sweet under our pillow. Then she would walk away, saying out loud, 'I've just put a sweet under X's pillow.' Time would elapse and inevitably X would root for the sweet. The staff member would pounce on her, shouting, 'I knew you weren't asleep' and firmly bash her by pushing her head deep into the pillow. It was a clever ploy and we always fell for it. I suppose it's called living in hope!

Another, more damaging ploy used to hurry us up and get us into bed fast, was the staff telling us that the devil was down in the toilets. They would say in menacing tones: 'Don't you dare get out of that bed. If you do, the devil will get you.' We took that very seriously because we were being taught to believe in the power of the devil and we were really afraid.

There was a brown radio on the top of one of the cubicles. The staff slept in cubicles at both ends of the dormitory. That first night, I recall listening to what was to become a ritual – the shipping forecast as it went around every one of the sea areas of the country, from Malin Head to Mizen Head. Like a chant, the phrases 'one thousand and one millibars, falling slowly, one thousand and one millibars, rising slowly ...' are indelibly marked in my brain. As I listened intently to the forecast that night, and hundreds of nights afterwards, images of the sea, boats, fog and gales crowded my mind. It sounded like a forecast from a completely different planet. Lying there, my brothers were very much on my mind. I worried about them. I did not know what was happening to any of us. But I sensed that we had, in a way, been jailed. With this thought I fell asleep.

Some hours later I was awakened to be told that I had to go to the toilet. This was done to all of us in rotation. The idea behind waking us twice in the night, at 11.00pm and 2.00am, was to try to ensure that we didn't wet the bed. Many of us did anyway because we had had the hell scared out of us just before going to sleep. So waking us twice a night didn't make any difference whatsoever. For some reason, this didn't dawn on the nuns or the staff. It was a horrible ritual and involved much suffering for us. We were pushed, shoved and beaten towards the toilets, the staff in bad humour, we children half asleep.

Mostly, we sat two to a toilet, to speed up the process. There were potties round the edge of the toilets for smaller children. They often fell asleep on them and the potties keeled over. The staff would pull them by the hair and force them back into an upright position. These utterly distressed children cried and slipped on the urine-flooded floors, as they made their way back to their beds, with soaking wet feet. This is a sight I have never forgotten.

In an attempt to comfort myself, I used to sink deep into the hole of my mattress and bite my toenails. I was able to do this for many months, and then one night, to my horror, I discovered I couldn't reach my toes anymore. It was a huge disappointment and I was shocked. I remember trying all sorts of manoeuvres to reach my toes but to no avail. I began to bite my fingernails and the skin from the tops of them after this. I also developed a very serious skin problem on my left foot. It began as a small rash and soon developed into a huge one that covered my entire foot. It became very itchy and lasted for months. Within days of it developing I wasn't able to walk and was confined to bed for a while.

The orphanage doctor used to come occasionally to check it. A member of staff came every day with her bowl of scalding water, her scissors and her aluminium tin with gauze in it to change the dressing. She was the only person I saw all day, with a few exceptions. Food was a major issue and I used to wonder if anybody would remember to bring me my tea. I never minded if they forgot me at dinner time as I hated the food anyway. In fact, I prayed they would. That prayer was often answered and I was happy if they remembered me at tea time. Still, it was great to be out of school, and I'd be thinking about the other children having to endure that. On balance, I was glad to be sick.

During those early days in the dormitory, I listened to every sound. I could hear voices but not the conversations coming from the front hall, immediately beneath me. Although I was too far from the windows to see out, I knew when it was light and dark. Nobody thought to allow my brothers to come and visit me and I'd only see them by chance, as they passed my bed, en route to their own. We were like strangers. I didn't see my mother or father either. I don't know if they asked to see me and weren't allowed. As I lay there I used to hear them when they came to visit my brothers. My father used to give my brothers sweets for me and my mother would leave things for me like cardboard dolls with paper clothing which had flaps to keep them in place. I enjoyed dressing the dolls.

Sometimes other girls put themselves at great risk by sneaking up to the dormitory to say hello or loan me a comic. Our favourites were *The Beano* and *The Bunty*. I liked the 'Toots' character in particular. She reminded me of ourselves, with her short hair cut straight across, and somehow always finding herself in trouble. Mini the Minx and Roger the Dodger were great fun too. I spent much of my time, though, thinking about the past and wondering when we as a family were going home.

I realised quite quickly that we would not be going out to play around the corner with our friends, like we used to, and naturally I missed this very much. I had mixed feelings about not living with my parents. I was somewhat relieved to be away from the problems of home, most of which centred around the lack of money. Of course my mother was a very good manager of money when she had it. She was also an excellent cook, and we were never hungry. She baked her own bread, knitted and made our clothes. On a practical level, all we needed was a permanent home and some financial support.

Having said that, life at home was no bed of roses either. When Christopher, our youngest brother, was only a few days old my mother collected us on her way home from the hospital. On arrival, my father wasn't home and she had no money for heating. My mother was obviously very upset and was crying. I don't recall what happened immediately after that, but it's an event in our home life which impacted on me. Another incident concerning the unreliability of my father occurred the Christmas before we entered Goldenbridge. This particular evening we children, all washed and ready for bed, sat listening to Christmas songs on the radio while waiting up for my father. We waited and waited. Eventually he arrived and my mother was really upset because he was so late. She was even more upset, and indeed so were we, when she realised he'd forgotten to buy our promised treat. A major argument followed and I can still see my mother as she reached for the dishes behind her and threw them at him. We were really frightened as the dishes flew but I don't remember if they hit anyone.

While I did not lament the loss of this kind of stress, I very much missed other things of our home life, especially the freedom of playing and enjoying myself outside our house. It wasn't that my mother was neglectful when she let us out to play, but my twin Michael and I used to sneak out the gate and explore our environment. My aunt, who regularly visited, used to catch us and bring us home, but we continued to do it. My mother used to say I was a tomboy. She would send me out to play, sparkling clean and dressed prettily with ribbons in my hair. I used to return black from head to toe, because I had been playing with our neighbours on the railway track nearby.

My mother was a religious and pious woman in the sense that she took religious duties seriously. She insisted on dressing us in our 'Sunday best' for mass. She brushed my hair and styled it as if she were preparing me for a party. I hated this ritual because it hurt and I didn't like the green silky ribbons which she put on my hair. But we always had to look our very best entering the house of God. She had respect for the

Church and often took us to the Carmelite church in Whitefriar Street where the large entrance porch was adorned with many statues of the saints. She prayed to these saints, especially St Jude, the patron saint of hopeless cases.

Like so many mothers of the era, she sent me to Irish dancing classes which I enjoyed until she insisted that I show her what I had learned. When, in my effort to impress her, I danced eagerly across the sitting room and continued into the kitchen, she laughed at me and I lost all interest in Irish dancing.

As a child I had a tendency to faint and one day my mother heard a doctor say on the radio that children who fainted regularly were seeking attention. She obviously believed him, and when he advised his audience that the only way to stop children fainting was to beat it out of them, she did what the doctor suggested. It didn't, of course, stop me fainting, but it allowed her to vent her own spleen on many occasions, and I didn't like that at all.

My mother wasn't slow about putting burdens on me at home. I used to think that because I was a girl she expected me to be more responsible than my brothers. I remember one day she commanded me, with finger pointing, not to forget to get off the bus at the correct stop. On this particular misty day all went well on the way and we went into the shop beside St Anne's, our school in Milltown, bought sweets and walked along by the narrow wall which ran past the garage beside the school.

Then on the way home things went badly wrong. I can still recall the terror that welled up inside me when I wiped the window to discover we had passed our stop. I jumped up from my seat, called my brothers to the platform and without looking, jumped off the bus, urging them to jump too. Thankfully they didn't. I ended up in a heap on the road, lucky not to have been killed. The bus conductor carried me home in his arms while my brothers, looking very glum, walked alongside us. I'll never forget the fear as we approached home. I pleaded with the conductor not to tell my mother what I had done. Thankfully, I don't remember what happened next.

Bad and all as these things were, it was little compared to what was in store for me and my brothers at Goldenbridge.

CHAPTER TWO

– Mornings in Hell –

My first full day in Goldenbridge orphanage began with noise and lots of hustle and bustle. We were woken at 6.00am to the aggressive switching on of lights. The loud thud was so sudden, we were literally frightened out of our sleep. This introduction to the day was angry and vindictive. Lay staff fulfilled the task of getting us up, and aggressively pulled bedclothes off us, and if we didn't move quickly enough they would often give us a stinging slap to waken us more promptly. In the beginning I found this absolutely shocking.

The staff seemed always to be alert and fully in their stride, shouting and lashing out viciously at whichever child happened to cross their path. They regularly beat us at this hour of the morning for no reason at all. It was as if they were totally resentful of our existence and at our being such a nuisance to them. We children, upset and crying, dressed ourselves as quickly as we could. Those who were old enough set about tidying and cleaning the dormitories. We made our own beds and then pulled them, heavy as they were, to the middle of the dormitory. We swept floors, dusted and then returned the beds to their original position, without marking the floor or making a sound.

A large wickerwork basket was brought to the top of the dormitory for wet sheets, of which there were plenty. The stench of urine and the very tense atmosphere created in the dormitories made our unhappiness complete. Those of us who wet the bed were given a very difficult time by the staff, who

22

called us all sorts of names, beat us and told us to go to St Patrick's. This was the order we all dreaded. It meant waiting for a nun who slapped and battered myself and other 'wet-the-beds', as we were called. This might have something to do with the fact that in centuries past it was believed that whipping cured everything from fevers to wetting the bed. Whatever people thought in the past, it was perfectly obvious to me as a child of 7 years of age, living in the Goldenbridge of the 1960s, that it didn't work. That's why I couldn't understand why they continued the humiliations, punishment beatings and 'leathering'.

For some reason, the lay staff employed to work in the orphanage were called teachers, though they weren't actually teachers. I don't know what they were really supposed to do, but it seems that they were there to supervise us. But their main objective, it seemed to me, was to make us ultra submissive, so that we did everything instantly and without question. Some of them achieved this by inflicting as much physical, mental and emotional pain as they were capable of. In this they were extremely clever and very creative. I believe it's nothing short of a miracle that some of them didn't literally kill us.

Those of us who had already made our holy communion set off for 7.00am mass in the nuns' chapel. En route, we collected our mantillas, then, in a straight line, marched in silence to the cloister. This was an outdoor roof attached to the convent roof and we stood under it, in all weathers, and without coats, until the lights of the priest's Volkswagon appeared in the distance. The registration number of his car I recall was BIN. His arrival signalled it was time for us to enter the chapel. This procedure ensured that we never arrived before him, so he didn't need to feel bad about being late, or about our getting soaking wet on wet, windy mornings.

Once inside the chapel, in the early mornings, our eyes would sting from the cold and the strong lights. We took our seats, not daring to look back at the nuns, who sat immediately behind us. We used to remark to one another that in this place, 'you couldn't look crooked'. The chapel was certainly one place we didn't dare look anywhere but straight ahead.

Mass would begin and at regular intervals the thud of one of us hitting the hard wooden floor would be heard. Our eyes, but not our heads, would look in the direction of the sound and we felt sorry for whoever had fainted. This happened a lot because we were tired and hungry, having fasted from supper time at 6.00pm the previous day. Fainting did not endear us to the nuns – one nun in particular used to be livid. She was forever saying that we 'let her down' in front of the nuns in the convent. Some children fainted more than others and one girl in particular fainted almost every day. Another nun used to place this girl between herself and another child who was known never to faint, so that they could prop her up when she began to get weak. It usually didn't work, but such was the nuns' concern about it that they went to those lengths rather than allow the poor child to rest in bed.

The need of a toilet was always a problem for younger children in the chapel but we couldn't leave. Naturally, some were unable to control the urge and in desperation wet ourselves. The nuns used to be furious and humiliated us for doing such a dirty thing in God's house. As with so many other things, the nuns always expected us to behave as if we were adults.

This was illustrated one morning when a young boy, who had just made his first communion, was caught handling and eating a communion wafer. He was well and truly shamed for committing such a crime. The nuns said he was now in a state of mortal sin and had a big black stain on his soul. We felt really scared for him, but he was a spirited child who didn't seem too concerned that his soul was no longer spotless. I recall being very confused, and I've no doubt others were too, about what to do when the communion wafer got stuck on the roof of my mouth. None of us dared ask. We didn't know if we could touch it with our tongue, and so were never quite sure if we too were in a state of mortal sin.

The mass itself was beyond our comprehension, as it was said entirely in Latin. It felt like a meaningless and boring ritual we just had to go through. I used to kneel, whiling away the time, observing the priests, who seemed big and over-fed. The chaplain, who was young, slim and good looking, was the exception. The rest were doddery, retired priests and their masses were always much longer. They wore very ornate religious garments with lots of fine, colourful needlework, and the letters IHS on their back. We used to think the letters stood for 'I have suffered' and we could easily identify with those words. But there wasn't any sign that the nuns and staff were suffering.

I stared at the statues, one of the Sacred Heart with a big red heart, and another of Our Lady standing on a serpent. They used to tell us that the serpent was the devil but I couldn't understand how the devil was a snake and I couldn't understand why Our Lady had no shoes when she was otherwise dressed so well. A huge crucifix over the altar, with the letters INRI, helped pass a lot of time. I tried to make up words for the letters but I never succeeded.

I spent much of the time in the chapel trying to find a comfortable spot to lean on. I used to wish I was tall enough to rest my elbows or even my head on the bench, which seemed so high above me. Being so small I couldn't even see over the rail and anything I did see was through the large gap in the bench. We weren't even allowed to lean back on the seats so it was very uncomfortable to have to kneel and sit straight for so long. When mass was finally over we marched as before in single file back to the orphanage and the work of the day.

St Joseph's, The Babies' Dormitory

We went straight from the chapel to St Joseph's to dress the babies and tidy and clean the dormitory. One of the older orphans would be put in charge of the babies, helped by us. The girls chosen for this job spent practically all the time, seven days a week, with them, without the help of any of the staff. St Joseph's dormitory was dark and miserable, with room for about 20 cots. Located on the top floor, near the nuns' cells, it led to the back stairs, a hiding place for us when we wanted to avoid yet another religious ceremony. It was airless, with a strong smell of urine and always seemed to be in semi-darkness, even though it had six large windows.

Babies were strapped to their potties for long periods of time. The poor babies often sat there so long that they fell asleep and their potties keeled over. It was a very unpleasant job cleaning up, but it was a job that had to be done whether or not we liked it.

There were steps at the side of some of the cots which were made specially for us to stand on because we were too small to reach into the cots. We helped get the babies ready and then cleaned their dormitory as well. I remember too that when we were woken to go to the toilet at night, some of the girls had to go to St Joseph's and help get the babies up to go to the toilet as well.

I have mentioned that Christopher, my youngest brother, was a baby when we came to Goldenbridge. One of the things that still disturbs me is that, for some reason, I don't recollect seeing him among the other babies in St Joseph's. I know rationally that he was there. I recall in detail what he looked like, from the freckles on his skin to the smile on his face, and the details of his clothes. I also recall his temperament, behaviour and personality as a baby but, curiously, I associate all of the memories with him in the company of our mother on Sundays when she came to visit or take us out. Perhaps remembering him as an infant without his mother is more than I can bear. All the same, it upsets me and in the past it induced severe guilt in me because I felt I must have abandoned him in that awful environment. This is one of the many painful legacies of living in Goldenbridge that I have had to come to terms with.

Goldenbridge Breakfast

The dining-hall seemed enormous and looked like an army mess. It must have been big because it seated over 200 of us. The 'big end' adjoined the kitchen while at the 'little end' there was a constant smell of bread from the pantry nearby. The floor had a speckled pattern with large black squares which made it seem dirty even though we scrubbed it thoroughly every day. Brightly painted blue presses ran along the side wall. When opened, the insides revealed the original dark brown paint of the past. I always tried to avoid storing dishes because that colour never failed to depress me. I imagined previous generations of children having to look at it every day. This might explain why, to this day, I associate the colour with institutional life. The furniture was the usual institutional type, wooden with formica surfaces and steel legs, where we sat six to a table.

The ritual at breakfast as at all meals was to stand for 'grace', a prayer before meals, usually led by a nun, followed by the clamouring of noise, when the big girls and staff served cocoa from huge pots. Although the plastic dishes were brightly coloured, the cups always smelled of soup.

Breakfast, like almost everything in Goldenbridge, meant a lot of work and little eating. The food was hardly worth the effort required, and I used to sometimes think it would have been kinder not to feed us at all. Preparation was very heavy work, however. For example, we would have to lift large aluminium churns of milk up 10 high steps, and into the huge freezer in the scullery. This was a job more suited to two strong men, but we struggled with them, even in very icy conditions, all the time terrified that they would fall over and spill. It was a job that we hated, not least because we could not get the heat back in our hands and we'd be frozen for the rest of the day.

Breakfast was simple, consisting of cocoa, bread and cold porridge, with lumps sometimes as big as golf balls. It was usually prepared by one of the staff who had been raised in Goldenbridge. The porridge was sometimes laced with sugar and tasted nice if we could avoid the lumps. More often it was covered with salt, especially if the staff were in bad humour, and some of them often were.

We made deals with each other at breakfast. We'd ask someone to eat our lumpy porridge in exchange for our quota of bread, and this system worked quite well. It was one of the fairest systems in operation at Goldenbridge. Occasionally, we resorted to distracting the child sitting next to us and dumped our lumpy porridge on her plate. That wasn't very nice of us but it wasn't as cruel as the behaviour of the adults around us.

Many of us, for years after leaving Goldenbridge, couldn't stand the sight of porridge, and one person told me recently that the sight of a man's 'Adam's apple' continues to remind her of Goldenbridge porridge. On that note, while shopping in a supermarket recently, I was amused to find a cereal called Goldenbridge Muesli for sale. I resisted buying it because it conjured up strong images and memories of Goldenbridge porridge. Reflecting on it later, I decided it was silly to allow that association to get in the way of trying a new cereal. Having made up my mind to challenge myself in this small way, I found that the product wasn't available at the original source. Undaunted, I traced the manufacturers and they sent me a complimentary pack which I thoroughly enjoyed. So Goldenbridge cereals, once a bad story, had a happy ending for me!

Bread was seriously rationed to two slices per person, per

meal, and sometimes it was mouldy. We'd pick the blue mould off it but didn't always succeed in removing the taste of it. We ate it because it was tolerable and we were hungry. Occasionally there was a shortage of bread, and I recall that there was a long bread strike during a winter in the mid-60s. Quite often, bread was the only food that we liked in the day, and we hated when it arrived late.

Kennedy's supplied our bread, and they advertised heavily on the radio with a catchy tune which we happily sang along with though we didn't always agree, especially with the last bit: K for Kennedy, E for energy, N for nice and nourishing, E for enjoyment, D for delicious, Y S means you're satisfied.

The Washroom

After breakfast came the washing ordeal. The washroom was a thoroughly miserable place, like something straight out of a Charles Dickens novel. It was an ancient, cold and extremely damp environment, a place we absolutely hated. I can still recall the tense atmosphere in it. What seemed like hundreds of washhand basins lined the walls. The floor was always slippy and wet from spillage and some of us had nasty falls. Soon after arrival in Goldenbridge we were given our very own patterned plastic washbag in which we kept our toothbrush, paste and facecloth.

One of the few things we could call our own was our identity number. All our underwear was labelled with this number, and we were often referred to by our number rather than our name. It felt strange to be called by a number: mine was 138. I never felt comfortable responding to it. I couldn't understand the need for a number because in the ten years I was there, I don't recollect that any two children had the same name. It was a demeaning, cruel but effective way to help us lose our identities. As a result, some of the very small children didn't even know their names.

The staff supervised us washing and one of the harshest treatments they subjected us to was a sudden and stinging slap across the face, arms or legs for not washing fast enough. The force and pain of these slaps was shocking and painful because the cloth or towel they beat us with was wet. Some of the staff were so rough that we often gave them nicknames that referred to their rough hands or strong arms.

One of the things we had in common with 'outsiders' was the fine-combing of hair. Unlike many of them, though, our experience was yet another opportunity for the staff to hurt and humiliate us. They stood at the top of the room with a fine-comb in one hand and a piece of cardboard in the other. We stood in a long line waiting our turn. They used so much pressure that the fine-comb often got stuck in our heads, scratching and sometimes cutting the scalp. We learned to turn slowly but surely in a circle until we got the signal, a firm punch on the head, which indicated that the fine-combing ordeal was over. Those of us who were unfortunate enough to have head lice were called all sorts of names which made us feel so ashamed. Punishment was the order of the day for this as well as for everything else over which we had no control. Along with the beating, the staff used to put Lorexene, a thick, oily substance with a strong smell, on our hair. We hated that because the other children avoided us and some of them called us names. Sometimes the staff or the nuns shaved our heads, the ultimate treatment which we dreaded.

Washing was the time of day when 'specials' or 'pets' were clearly distinguishable from the rest of us. Specials were children who were the favourites of the orphanage. There were about seven or eight at any one time, ranging in age from babies to sixteen. One of the many privileges of being a special was that the girls had ribbons put in their hair by their teacher or nun. The staff and nuns often bought them clothes, so they were dressed differently to the rest of us.

We used to tease the specials about the 'airplanes' in their hair, because the ribbons sat rigid on their heads like the wings of a plane. This never failed to upset them. Sometimes they reported us, but usually they had more sense than to do that. I know now they must have suffered for their privileged positions, but because we were children who were treated so badly by the adults who loved them, we didn't appreciate that at the time. It looked and seemed to us that they were having an easy life, and we isolated and bashed them when we got the chance. The staff used to say we were envious, and perhaps we were. That doesn't alter the fact that as adults and members of staff, they should have avoided favouritism.

The Laundry

Mondays and Fridays were laundry days, and we pulled large wickerwork baskets of soiled linen all the way from the orphanage to the laundry. The baskets had huge leather straps on the lids and when the teachers were out of sight we happily kicked the baskets down the stairs. This made the job easier and gave us some fun. Often, we put each other in, secured the belts and shoved them down the stairs. This was great fun unless we were unlucky enough to come tumbling out and landed hard on the stairs, bruising and hurting ourselves. We didn't complain of our injuries no matter how painful because we ran the risk of getting some more bruises as punishment. Once the fun was over, laundry days were very hard work.

We dragged the baskets past the front of the convent, an uphill journey from the orphanage, past the chapel, then shoved them downhill past the secondary school, and into the laundry. Girls over twelve were taken out of school and did most of the laundry work from 9.30am to lunch time.

First the sheets were boiled in huge vats, which created masses of steam and very damp conditions. They were then rinsed by hand, in cold water. I remember working in the laundry on Saturday mornings, lifting the sheets from the vats with long wooden tongs that had a steel grip. We liked climbing the ladders to reach the wooden slats, which we called 'horses', for hanging the sheets. I'll never forget the sight of the girls coming back from the laundry, with soaking wet shoes which looked so uncomfortable.

The Classroom

Perhaps because it felt like we were in prison, I wasn't surprised to discover that Goldenbridge orphanage had its own school inside the orphanage. It was separate and distinct from Goldenbridge National and Secondary schools, for outsiders. These schools, just a stone's throw from the orphanage, were also run by the Sisters of Mercy. They were in the convent grounds but for some unknown reason we weren't allowed to attend them. The nuns provided the best of free education for children living in the Inchicore area, and they were very proud of the fact that they were innovative in providing free secondary education.

We attended our own school, though some years later when free education was introduced for all by the Government, I was one of the privileged few from the orphanage who attended the secondary school. For that I am forever grateful. Going to school inside the orphanage meant that we rarely saw other children and later this made it difficult for us to mix easily with our peers in the secondary school.

There were only two trained teachers, and they came in from outside. A nun taught girls over 12, when she was available, while another nun taught the infant classes. My twin, Michael, and I were put into the joint first and second class, my next brother went into high infants and Christopher was put into Guardian Angels, the babies' room.

St Brigid's, our classroom, with its large windows, faced onto the Grand Canal. About 60 of us sat two to a desk which were made of heavy oak attached to curved wrought-iron legs. Each desk contained two inkwells with copper lids. The dark walls were adorned with pictures depicting the Joyful, Glorious and Sorrowful Mysteries of the Rosary. Posters from which we learned Irish and English also decorated the walls. Ten times tables which we learned by rote hung there too.

Almost everything else we learned throughout the years in school was about people who didn't live in orphanages, people like mammies, daddies and their children who lived together in houses. I felt sad when we learned about these children playing with cats and dogs in their own gardens, the kinds of things we did before we were brought to Goldenbridge. I didn't tell anyone about my thoughts and feelings because I was afraid I might upset them. But the stories of children going to the shops to buy food and sweets did remind me of life at home and I missed my old school which was much nicer than this one. We learned about Oliver Twist and his was the only life that seemed real to me now that I was living in Goldenbridge. His life was so like ours because he was hungry and adults were always cruel to him too.

Writing with the left hand was a most serious offence. Those of us who did were called *citeógs* and teachers used to say that we were doing the devil's work and were evil. This really scared me. One of them tried with all her might to literally beat this habit out of us. As she passed us she slapped us across the ears, pucked our elbows and bashed our desks, shouting, 'I'll knock the devil out of you.' We were terrified and lots of us would be crying at the same time but the teacher was steadfast and relentless in her determination to succeed in making us write with our right hand.

My twin Michael and myself were left-handed but I adjusted very quickly to writing with the right hand, unlike Michael who was much slower to change. I was in agony when the teacher focused her attention on him, while I wished to

God he would just do as she told him. I can see now that I began to think like her because I too became angry and frustrated with him for not learning faster. I can still see the strain on his face.

One teacher's speciality was to make us stand while she poked the backs of our thighs with a stick as she screamed, 'I'll write your name in blood.' Because we were so scared and frightened few of us could retain much of what she taught us. Sometimes we knew the lesson for the day and then forgot it completely. No doubt this frustrated her, and as she was liberal with her stick it gave her another excuse to use it. She also used a ruler and to ensure that she hurt us as much as possible, she used the side of it to slap us. If we withdrew our hand, as was natural, in anticipation of the pain, it hurt much more because the stick caught the ends of our fingers. For attempting to withdraw our hand, she'd give us twice as many slaps.

This woman did not seem to understand children, and didn't seem to care that she was adding to our misery. The cause of our inability to learn was that we were exhausted, hungry and sad. We were emotionally and physically wrecked from the hard work we did before coming to school. In addition, we were trying to cope with extraordinary levels of cruelty, inside and outside the classroom.

In another class the teacher ruled us with her stick. This stick had an interesting history. One of the boys stole it after class one day and threw it over the wall in the backyard beside the canal. We were delighted but at the same time anxious in case she ever found out who did it. Next day we arrived in class and the stick was there as usual. We never found out whether she found it on her way to school or whether she had a replacement stick in reserve. She never mentioned the fact that the stick had gone missing. We lived in dread of that stick.

By the time I progressed into fifth class things were changing in Goldenbridge. We had a brand new school, a very bright, airy, clean building, with tall windows. We could see and hear the children in the separate national school, less than 100 yards from us. The Minister for Education, Donogh O'Malley, visited us. Our teachers in fifth and sixth class were new to the school and showed some signs of humanity and good humour. These teachers were young and attractive and on the whole we got on fairly well with them.

While in sixth class I sat the state examination, the Primary Certificate. A supervisor was assigned to our class. We filled our date of birth and the examination date in spaces provided. As the supervisor passed me, she told me in no uncertain terms that it was my date of birth she wanted, not today's date. I explained rather feebly that this was my birthday and she softened for a moment as she said, 'I hope you have a nice day.' Then she punched me hard on the shoulder and said, 'Now, get on with your work.' I was perplexed and felt very hurt by this and it took me a while to settle down to the exam. I asked myself why I felt so hurt, when I'd never met her before. I think, in retrospect, it was because she was from 'outside' and I had expected her to behave more kindly towards me.

During the exam, one of the nuns kept wandering in and out of the classroom and walking around helping us with our sums and Irish. She went so far as to write sample Irish answers up on the board, in the presence of the supervisor. She told us we weren't all to write the same thing and that some of us were to change words round a bit. As far as I know, we all passed the Primary Certificate that year!

Dinner

Some of the girls in my class, even though they were young and small at age 8 or 9, were taken out of class to help the big girls prepare the dinner. A friend of mine was always taken out to wash and clean the vegetables in the ante-room at the back of the orphanage, which was bitterly cold. Her skin cracked and became sore, itchy and bloody. Nobody seemed to notice until the medical inspector came and he referred her to Hume Street Hospital, where she was admitted. She spent what she describes as 'the best and happiest three months' of her childhood there. The nurses and doctors were very kind to her and although she never had any visitors, other children's parents and the nurses brought her sweets and lemonade. She sobbed when she was told that they were sending her back.

On entry to the dining room for dinner, it was easy to tell whether we were in for a treat or what we called slops. Dinner was by far the worst of the three meals. The stench of stew as it was poured from the jugs made us nauseous.

Delicate children got goody, which was bread soaked in milk and sweetened with sugar, and we were envious of them. Some also got Liga and we were even more envious of them, so much so, we resorted to robbing it from them. It tasted so delicious and was so thick and so filling, we wished we could be delicate too. The non-delicate among us sometimes got mashed potatoes which were lumpy, grey and cold. Thinking of them now makes me want to throw up, and that's what would happen to us a lot. Occasionally, we got lime-coloured soup, corned beef and suet. The only vegetables I remember getting were turnips, carrots and what we called 'swimming' cabbage. Curiously, we always got dessert. Sago, which we called rubber balls, stuck to our fingers, hair, and even our clothes. We liked rice and semolina when they weren't lumpy and cold, but they nearly always were. Lumpy custard, brown and pink Farola, also made us gag but we were always forced to eat it.

One staff member in particular kept us back to finish dinner and dessert. This was extremely unpleasant, to say the least. Naturally, the colder it became, the more difficult it was to eat. We became pallid and sickly, as well as tearful and visibly upset. It was awful to see children vomiting their food and then being beaten for this too.

On the rare occasions that we did get good food, for instance on Sundays, we bartered it. Usually we got mince which, though greasy, was a little more palatable. When others were unwell, we didn't have to barter and simply begged, 'Give us your leavings, will ya?' Full or hungry, there followed clean-up time, which was another ordeal to be faced in the long days at Goldenbridge.

Cleanliness, Next to Godliness!

Clean-up after dinner, as you might imagine, was a very messy task. What seemed like thousands of plates and millions of pieces of cutlery had to be taken to the dishwasher and the tables and floor scrubbed. We worked in organised teams cleaning and arranging furniture in preparation for sweeping and scrubbing the floor. Buckets of soapy water were liberally thrown on the floor by a staff member. Puddles would flow, creating all sorts of shapes as they went their merry way. We scrubbed the floors with deck scrubs, while others followed with floorcloths and heavy aluminium buckets, to lift the excess water. Our hands and fingers became sore from wringing floorcloths. We often ended up with raw hands, cut fingers and blisters. A staff member would then check for cleanliness. Nothing short of meticulous perfection would do. Once she was satisfied, it was time for us to butter the bread and store it in large aluminium containers in readiness for supper, our evening meal. If we got the chance, and we rarely did, we robbed some and put it up our sleeves, sticky and all as it was, for later.

Sometimes our work in the dining-hall wasn't up to standard and we were punished for this by having to repeat the whole process. This caused much resentment and led to incidents which could easily have been avoided. One such incident concerned a girl who was very upset and angry about this. When she protested, a staff member beat her severely in front of us. She started by pulling her hair out by the roots, near her ears, which is extremely painful. She also beat her with the deck scrub and finally the girl retaliated. The fight spread onto the corridor outside the dining-hall until a nun arrived on the scene, to find us all standing around, watching. This incident was the talk of the place for the rest of the day, but within 24 hours this girl had been transferred to a reformatory school in Limerick. This place, run by the Sacred Heart nuns, had a fearsome reputation in Goldenbridge and we were constantly threatened with being sent there. The decision to transfer the girl was, in our minds, an unfair decision, but I've heard since that she found it less harsh and cruel than Goldenbridge.

This incident was typical of the kind of behaviour some staff engaged in: vindictive, punitive and abusive in the extreme. They had all the power while we had none. We couldn't protest about the unreasonable demands and behaviour of staff without running the risk of being transferred to a reformatory school. Under the rules pertaining to industrial schools, it seems the nuns did have the power to transfer us, with the permission of the Department of Education, for being disobedient. In practice, no such constraints were put on staff. They usually kept their jobs, regardless of the fact that they too had broken the rules governing discipline and punishments.

One staff member hated it when we didn't understand what she said, which happened frequently. One day, she told a girl who was helping prepare dinner for the teachers to tell two of the staff that their dinner was on the table. This girl mentioned to another girl that the staff member had said, 'I want margarine and marmalade on the tables.' The second girl, who knew the routine better, immediately realised that this was not the correct instruction. Realising the implications of this, the first girl begged the second not to tell the staff member that she had misunderstood her. She agreed, but later rescinded on her agreement and told. When the first girl returned from

delivering the correct instruction, the staff member was waiting for her and beat her badly around the head with a wet
floorcloth, shouting, 'You stupid child.' That wasn't the end of
the matter: the child was later ordered to scrub the dining-hall
floor, alone. Of such petty matters a great issue would often be
made in Goldenbridge.

These kinds of injustices evoked great anger in me at the
time. When a particularly harsh staff member was in the same
room as me, I found that I literally couldn't breathe I was so
scared and angry. This was a woman who, if she disliked or
found fault with anyone, seemed incapable of controlling her
contempt. In those situations she had absolutely no respect for
limb or life, though on occasions she was capable of having
favourites, whom she treated very well indeed. I used to
threaten staff members in my head, swearing that one day: 'I'll
be stronger than you. You just wait. I'll wait till I'm absolutely
sure I can beat you. Then I'll fight you and you'll be sorry.'

This was daily life in Goldenbridge, a blend of continuous
hard work, tough punishment and the constant fear of beatings. This was what I and my brothers had to get used to in the
early weeks in the orphanage. It was to become our way of life
for all the years we remained there.

CHAPTER THREE

– The Monkey and the Beads –

On sunny days we went to the yard to play after dinner and chores. It was surrounded on all sides by big grey buildings and walls, so high they prevented sunlight from entering the yard. This made for a cold, dreary atmosphere even on warm days. Katherine Behan, mother of the writer Brendan Behan, spent seven years of her childhood in Goldenbridge, beginning in 1898, and she described the yard in much the same terms. We didn't wear cardigans or socks in the summer, and because the yard was so cold, one of our favourite pastimes was to compete with others to see who had the most goose-pimples. The cold was compensated for to some extent by the fact that we loved our summer dresses, with their huge big pockets, because we could carry our possessions, the tools of playtime, around with us.

The building which housed the furnace was in the yard and we so dreaded this that some of us learned, for good reasons, to blank it from our memories. It was a forbidding-looking building on the outside but it was also a miserable, dark and lonely place on the inside. Many an adult who was raised in Goldenbridge remembers being pushed down the steps into it, screaming for mercy. Some who were punished in this way now feel that it later caused them to suffer serious reactions to confined spaces such as lifts and tunnels.

This furnace was a contentious issue on the 'Prime Time' television programme of April 1996 about Goldenbridge. I was astonished to watch the debate centre around how long a particular child had spent in the furnace. One person said she spent hours in the furnace while her sister argued she had spent 'only' minutes. I was truly amazed that nobody said that no child, under any circumstances, should ever be subjected to this form of punishment. In omitting to do this, they completely missed the point that this was a form of solitary confinement which was designed to hurt, isolate and terrify young children. It was certainly effective in achieving its aims and did untold long-term damage to its victims.

In contrast, the merry-go-round, which was beside the furnace, was cheerful, painted red and blue, with a wooden seat. We used to push it around while banging it against its centre pole of support. We did somersaults on it and often when it suddenly stopped, we badly grazed our knees and legs on the gravel. Occasionally, the enormous bolts which secured the seat bashed down on our knees, and this was sheer agony. When that happened, we were too afraid to say we'd hurt ourselves and our wounds and pains wouldn't be attended to. Oozing sore knees were common and some of the teachers must have noticed them. If they did, they didn't do anything about them, and I'd suggest that if they didn't notice these wounds, they must have been going round with their eyes closed. In any event, the wounds healed in the course of time.

On Sundays some of us went out with relatives or host families and brought back marbles and caps or bangers which made a great bang when bashed against the outside walls of the washroom. We loved to bring back marbles and caps, because both boys and girls liked them and could play with them together. Otherwise, I didn't get much chance to play with my brothers, because the boys didn't like playing skipping or hopscotch.

There was one incident in the yard with my twin, Michael, that I remember always. We were playing happily together when he told me he had sixpence. I asked him to share it with me, but he refused. I was disappointed and upset because I thought that his refusal meant he didn't love me. I pleaded with him and begged him, until finally he gave in. I knew in my heart and soul that he didn't want to give it to me, but it seemed very important to me that he did. Having forced the money from him, I didn't feel any more loved or cherished by him. Instead, I felt emotionally empty and ashamed. This testing of others remained a characteristic of significant relationships in my life, long after I left Goldenbridge. At the time of the incident with Michael, and for much of my adult life, I had an insatiable longing to be loved, affirmed and accepted. It seemed that when I was a small child, very few people, including myself, understood the depth, root and pain of these feelings and needs which are common to all children.

Provided we were left undisturbed by adults, playtime was some respite from the rest of the day. Usually, at this time of the day, we were left alone for about 20 minutes, but this applied only to dry days. Sometimes we got into trouble. One day, a boy brought chalk back from a day out with his family. He gave some to his friends and they were caught by one of the nuns, writing on the walls of the yard. She ordered them to clean it off with handbrushes and water. Since the boys didn't normally do manual work, we girls, who had been told not to help them, did. We too were caught by a nun and she beat us while she supervised the boys completing the work.

The swings which sat motionless that first day in the yard were always fully occupied when we were allowed to play. We became so skilled and creative using them! We pushed one another so high on them that anyone watching would think we were sure to go over the bars. We also sat astride them and, having put spare swings round the posts, we pushed the swing sideways. The heights we reached from this position were incredible. We turned the seats of the swings, over and over, until they were above our heads, then held ourselves up with the chains as the swing unfurled to its original position.

Sometimes when the swings reached their full height, we ran under them. This was a dangerous activity. The aim was to outwit the motion and speed of the swing. A challenge, which didn't always pay off, was to jump when the swing reached its full height. Once I jumped and I was horrified to see the wall of the food storage room come to meet me. I was lucky not to have split my head open. I never tried that stunt again.

At these times most of the teachers were having lunch in St Ita's, the staff dining room, which was a distance from the yard. It was wonderful for us to have time to enjoy ourselves with abandon. The nuns in charge of the orphanage were in the convent having lunch and reading their daily prayers from their breviaries. We used to see them and the other nuns walking round their garden, reading, as we cleaned after dinner. A wire fence separated the nuns' garden from the back of the orphanage, where trams belonging to CIÉ were stored. It was only at these times, or at film-shows and concerts, that we saw the faces of the other nuns in the convent. It didn't matter to us that they hardly ever spoke to us, because they rarely impacted on our lives, unlike the nuns who worked in the orphanage and would soon return.

One rather extraordinary inhabitant of Goldenbridge, Jenny, a rhesus monkey kept as a pet by one of the nuns, did impact on our lives. When this nun returned from the convent after dinner, she released the monkey from her cage in the front hall and brought her to the yard where we were playing. We didn't like Jenny much because, like her owner, she was fast-moving and pounced on us when we least expected it. This nun liked Jenny and was always very nice to her.

Because Jenny was a monkey, she didn't appreciate the fact that we didn't enjoy her chasing us around, pulling our hair and scratching us. We were young and scared and we thought Jenny was very rough. When we were caught defending ourselves against Jenny, we were punished. The nun took Jenny's side in everything and the monkey always won.

In retrospect, I don't think it was appropriate to have a monkey amongst so many small children. Apparently the monkey had been bought so that we would learn about how animals treated their young, and for sex education. This is very odd indeed, as we all know a lone monkey couldn't teach us much about sex education. On this issue, what I do recollect is that, because Jenny was alone, she masturbated on the sideboard in the dining-hall. I know, in practice, that what the nuns wanted to teach us about sex was to stay away from men. To that extent, Jenny may well have taught us something about not needing men for sexual gratification!

Scraps, Scraps!

We knew when the staff finished their lunch because the window at the top of the yard opened and the teachers shouted, 'Scraps, Scraps.' These were left-overs from staff meals and were thrown from a large enamel sieve. As they flew in all directions, we rushed forward to catch them. The scraps consisted of unfinished toast, bread, margarine, and if we were lucky, bits of cake and fruit. As we dived for the scraps, fights and squabbles broke out, and the little ones got hurt. When they did manage to grab some, the big girls sometimes took it from them, leaving them crying and upset.

Unfinished business was sometimes brought from the yard to the classroom and one such incident concerned a girl who had hidden bread and margarine up her sleeve. A teacher, not knowing this, went to slap her and when the girl tried to pull away from her, the margarine fell out of her sleeve. She then tried to run away from the teacher, who followed her and landed flat on her back with her feet in the air. While we were terrified of the consequences we just couldn't contain our laughter. I don't recall the teacher's reaction but I can imagine that I might have thought she deserved it and that, for a change, justice had been done.

For several weeks each year we got some respite from our own teachers. Student teachers came from the Sisters of Mercy Carysfort Teacher Training College. These were very nice young women and were kind to us. They never slapped or hurt us. We loved it when they came and they taught us all the usual subjects without fear or violence. As a result, we learned and retained what they taught us, at least until their inspectors had come and gone. The students were always nervous of the nun inspectors and they kept us informed about them. For instance, they told us which inspectors went harder on them than the others. We felt that they had some appreciation of our position, and while they never said so directly, we felt that they sided with us against both their and our oppressors. They knew how to get our co-operation, and were happy to negotiate with us. The students brought much pleasure and fun to the classroom, and on their last day at the school each year they gave us sweets and we sang the student song:

> Pounds, shillings and pence,
> The students have no sense,
> They come to school, to act the fool,
> Pounds, shillings and pence.

Making Rosary Beads

After school, our classroom was converted into the rosary beads manufacturing class. We worked as part of the manufacturing process for two factories, for a fee, though we received no payment apart from 2/6d on St Patrick's Day for the whole year's work – and this was withheld if we were not 'good'. At the age of 6 we began our training by learning how to string the beads, and within weeks we had progressed to learning how to make the beads. Two tins of beads were put on each desk. Two staff members were in charge of this class. The first thing we learned was to string the beads on to the appropriate wire. There were two types of wire, a shiny-surfaced one for pearl and glass beads, and a tougher, darker one, which left black marks on our hands, for plastic beads. We learned to cut the wire with a pliers. This was heavy and cumbersome for small children and was difficult to handle, especially for those who were left-handed. It dug into our hands. The imprint on my hand remained there for many years after I left Goldenbridge.

We didn't actually manufacture the beads. They came from the factory, already pierced with a hole at both ends. So did the wire, which came in reams. Having learned to string the beads, we had to become competent in handling and cutting the wire with the pliers. Then we learned to loop the wire into the beads. It was important to achieve consistency in shape and size. We were then ready to make the decades. As you may appreciate, this was quite skilled work which required great speed, if we were each to achieve the target of making 60 of these decades in the limited time allocated. So we were under extreme pressure and it didn't help that the wire cut deep into our left index finger. These wounds never got time to heal fully and the wire eventually settled in the gap. Perhaps because of the pressure we were under, we used to rock backwards and forwards as we made the beads. We probably thought the rhythm helped. Perhaps it helped relieve the monotony.

A radio was always on during beads class, which we liked, but the staff were as hard on us in this class as anywhere else and one of them thought nothing of sticking a pliers in our arms if she caught us talking as she moved up and down the room. The other was a reasonable, less violent person, but often threatened to tell on us and get us into trouble. Her mantra was, 'I'm going to tell Sr ... on you.'

We made different types of beads. Plastic were the easiest, and we tolerated glass, but we hated making pearl beads. Glass and pearl beads were much harder to thread and they splintered, often ending up in our eyes, which left us extremely sore and uncomfortable. But even with splinters in eyes, or cut fingers, we had to carry on until we completed the full quota. When we finished, feeling tired and hungry, we handed our work to the staff who checked it for errors. Often they threw the lot back at us, without telling us what the problem was, and we had to work it out for ourselves before we dared to hand it in again.

Despite our efforts to keep up with the work, sometimes the factory was late delivering wire or beads, and precious time was wasted. When the wire eventually arrived from Mitchell's or Walsh's beads factory, we all gave a cheer; not because we were delighted to do the work, but because there was some hope we might get to bed at a reasonable hour.

Cleaning up after the beads class was often given as a punishment. One day I got into trouble over something, now long forgotten. A particular nun told me to clean up after the beads class every night, until further notice, as punishment. So, at 12 years of age, every night, for almost a year, I pulled every one of the benches forward, swept and cleaned the room, and returned those heavy desks to their original position. In addition, I had to sort the beads, collect the wire and tidy the beads press. I used to be exhausted and close to tears with the sheer hard work of it and the loneliness of doing it all by myself. I wanted to go to bed and sleep, but that was out of the question. In the meantime, I cursed that nun under my breath and a huge well of resentment grew inside me, not just towards her, but also at the public. I had plenty of time to reflect and I often wondered if all the Holy Marys and Holy Joes who bought and used those beads ever thought about who made them, and the blood, sweat and tears that went into them.

One night, quite unexpectedly, this nun came into the beads class and asked me what I was doing. I reminded her that she had assigned me to this task, almost a year earlier, and it was obvious she had completely forgotten about it. She released me from the duty and while I was grateful for that, it didn't alleviate the resentment, or the sense of injustice I felt about the arbitrary nature of this kind of punishment, which was so common in Goldenbridge.

On St Patrick's Day, every year, we received our pay, if we were good. If we had misbehaved we got nothing. We felt hurt and deeply upset when this happened because we had worked so hard all year. For those who did get paid, the nuns provided a temporary sweet shop in the Rec where we spent most of the money on 'black jacks', 'cleeves', and 'fresher sweets', because they lasted longest.

I have to say, I still have negative feelings towards rosary beads. Many years later an acquaintance gave me a gift of a set, and suddenly the strength of my feelings became evident. I had never owned a set, and never had reason to use them. Such was my experience of rosary beads that it was extremely difficult for me to appreciate the gift in the spirit in which it was given.

At 5.40pm we got a break from making the beads to go to Benediction, a religious service which lasted about 20 minutes. I never had a clue what the service was about, but I recall the priest saying lots of prayers, and the nuns singing Latin hymns such as 'Tantum Ergo'. Not understanding Latin, we joined in the singing using our own words. For example, 'Watch my hair grow' rhymed with 'Tantum Ergo'. The priest carried the monstrance very reverently. It looked like a gold circle, surrounded by shining, gold, inverted 'sun-rays' which glistened with the strong lights of the chapel. This had a mesmerising effect on us who were so very tired. The priest always lit incense, which I found relaxing.

We especially didn't like Benediction on Mondays, because it was longer, owing to the perpetual novena to 'Our Lady of the Miraculous Medal' being added to the 'Litany of the Saints'. This was a prayer to which we responded 'pray for us' at the end of every sentence, until we were utterly blue in the face. A good friend of mine, like so many of us, got fed up with this pious practice, and occasionally she hid under bundles of mattresses to avoid it. One day she nearly smothered herself, after which she decided that the monotony of Benediction was preferable to dying of suffocation.

We then returned to the orphanage for tea, our favourite meal of the day. Though it was simple and consisted of two slices of bread and cocoa, there was little trauma attached to it. As usual, there was clean-up and preparation for the next morning's breakfast, but this was relatively easy and quickly achieved.

After tea, we sometimes watched TV and my favourite programme was 'Mr Ed'. It was about a talking horse. Being 7 years old at the time, I couldn't quite decide if a horse could talk. I was fascinated by the idea that maybe it could, but never asked anybody about it. Another of my favourite programmes was 'Marcus Welby MD'. He seemed such a gentle, kind man, that I often thought I'd love him to be my daddy.

When the staff became aware of programmes we liked, they made noise, dragging furniture, shouting at us and sending us on messages. We felt they were being vindictive, but we couldn't retaliate when the news, which they wanted to see, was on. Instead, we had to endure absolute silence.

Some of us lived for 'The Monkees' on Saturday nights. So we rushed through tea and clean-up, to get back to St Patrick's for 6.30pm while one of the staff, we felt, did all in her power to delay us. While we felt upset and angry about this, there was nothing we could do about it. These struggles, because they were never openly named and discussed, were truly exhausting.

CHAPTER FOUR

– Days of Judgement –

At one stage, I and my three brothers almost escaped the experience of Goldenbridge and long-term institutional life. To this day, I don't quite understand what went wrong. A few months after arriving in Goldenbridge, we were told by one of the nuns, quite suddenly one day, that we were going home 'for good'. We were delighted. All four of us stood in the front hall, coats on, waiting for our mother. Eventually she arrived and she and the nun spoke. I don't know what transpired between them, but the nun then made a phone call. When she put the phone down she turned to us and said: 'Take your coats off. You're not going home.' My mother was really upset and tried reasoning with her but to no avail. I was absolutely devastated, as we walked along the miserable, long, brown corridor, back to the yard. I still cringe at the memory of how embarrassed I felt when we returned to the yard. Everyone had thought we were going home. They had come to us and said, 'It's well for you, going home.' But there we were, back in the yard like everybody else. It was awful when they said, 'What's wrong? Why aren't you going home?' All I could do was shrivel up inside. I don't remember talking to my brothers about any of this at the time. I was too upset for myself and for them.

On 20 September 1962 there was another sudden announcement. 'The Fahys are going to court today. Get your coats.' We had no idea why we were going to court, but a staff member brought us in the nuns' car. It wasn't unusual for someone to be going to court, it's just that I had never expected it to happen to us. The children never talked about their court cases. They never said how they felt about court, but it usually ended with them having to stay in Goldenbridge until they reached the magical age of 16.

We arrived at the Children's Court in Dublin Castle and both my parents were there. It was a medium-sized dark room with loads of brown benches like we had in the Rec. The room was packed and I could barely see my parents who were seated on the other side of the courtroom. I don't recall that we talked to each other, but I definitely saw them. People stood up and spoke and then we went back to Goldenbridge. It was only a preliminary hearing and the case was adjourned. Three weeks later, on 11 October 1962, we were back in court, and our fate was decided.

This time we went with a senior member of staff and sat beside her at the back of the courtroom. Our mother was at the other side of the very packed room. Again, people spoke but I don't know what they said. The judge called us – myself and my brothers – up to his desk, which was on a podium. He was an oldish man with grey hair and he spoke to us gently. He asked us which of our parents we wanted to live with. I was shocked and bewildered by the question, but I sensed that the answer would be important. A rush of thoughts and feelings assailed me as I tried to think about it. I was busy imagining what it would be like to live with either of them separately, and I was also aware that I didn't want to hurt either of them. I knew too that the judge was waiting for our answer. I didn't know how to deal with that. I hadn't done all my thinking, though, when I heard my brothers say they wanted to live with our mother. I went along with that but I felt terribly guilty too about not choosing my father. I really wanted us to live with both of them and it felt very strange to be put in the position of choosing between them. I just wanted the court case to be over soon, so that we could all go home together. No sooner had we answered the question when the judge struck his desk with a gavel and announced that we were to be 'committed' to Goldenbridge until we each reached the age of 16. I understood exactly what this meant: we were not going home.

While this shocking news was sinking in, I was distracted by my brother wetting his pants. Whether he was shocked by the decision, or frightened by the unexpected striking of the gavel, I don't know, but certainly he reacted to something. He could clearly be heard and I was frightened when I looked down and saw a pool of water at the judge's feet. I was scared in case someone would bash him for it. Thankfully nobody did. While this went on, I was reeling with the implications of the decision. I fretted and cried, but I couldn't stop thinking about how on God's earth we would cope with this long 'sentence', a whole 10 years – more for the younger ones. It felt like we were being jailed.

I don't know why the judge put us through the ordeal of answering this question. In retrospect, I think his decision was a foregone conclusion and that the court case was a mere formality. I've wondered, too, what difference it might have made had we decided we wanted to live with our father. For many years I cursed that judge for the decision he made that day. I have thought a million times about whether or not he, and other judges with similar powers, knew the implications of their decisions.

I know now that after the preliminary hearing in court, the Gardaí at Kevin Street station became involved, for legal reasons. The records indicate that a Garda 'made enquiries and ascertained that these children were illegitimate'. He then served notice on the Dublin Health Authority. Their representative attended the adjourned case at which she offered no objection to our being committed. We were ordered to be detained in a certified industrial school, under Section 58(i)(h)(y) of the Children's Act of 1908-1957. We were committed by the courts, because of having 'a parent who does not exercise proper guardianship'.

My mother, rather than my father, for some reason, was ordered by the courts to pay 10 shillings, per child, per week, for the duration that we were detained. Within months, however, the Department of Education was writing to my father, seeking to have him pay the amounts due.

Separations and Losses

Separations were a fact of life for all of us in Goldenbridge. We all suffered the loss of our parents. I have only to cast my mind back to the arrival of new children in the orphanage to recall their grief. Children cried; siblings huddled together, looking bereft and shocked. No sympathy was offered to them by nuns or staff. Most often they grieved for a parent, usually their mother, who had just died. They were brought to the yard, dumped there, and were expected to carry on and participate in everyday routine events, as if nothing of any significance had happened to them. It was obvious to me, a mere child at the time, how cruel a practice this was. Things were done with an indifference to our feelings and this indifference amounted to cruelty.

In many cases, new children suffered the loss of their sisters or brothers as well. Boys could only stay in Goldenbridge until they were 10 years of age, so older brothers were usually sent to Artane. Children often lost contact with brothers throughout their stay in Goldenbridge. Sometimes contact was lost forever. None of the nuns – except for one of them – as well as the Christian Brothers in Artane and elsewhere, did anything to help siblings maintain contact. In fact, for some unknown reason, they seemed to actually discourage contact between family members in different institutions.

When new children arrived, particularly if they were sent by the courts, and were in bad health, their heads would be shaved and this was experienced as a very shameful event. I recall one group of siblings whose heads had been shaved in this way. They stood in the yard, from the smallest to the tallest, huddled together, shamed into silence, looking at us, the audience. The shaving was part of the 'medical' on entry to the orphanage. If they were unlucky, they had also to endure a dose of benzyl benzoate which had a very strong odour. This was known as the 'itch stuff', a treatment for scabies, a common childhood disease in those days.

Others stood, crying and sobbing their hearts out. We used to go up to them and say things like, 'You're new, aren't you?' 'What's your name?' 'What happened to your mammy?' Invariably this brought on more tears. Then we'd say, 'Don't worry, your mammy will come for you tomorrow.' We often invited them to come and sit or play with us but they would generally refuse and sit huddled together on the ground.

We were quite capable of being unkind to new children too, especially at night, when we put them through our initiation ceremony. Once they were assigned a bed, some of us would offer to make it for them. We made what we called a 'french bed', which meant folding the top sheet in two. When they got into bed, we heard the crack of their toes as they stretched their feet. It wasn't nice but it wasn't such a bad introduction to their stay in Goldenbridge.

Some staff were unkind to them too, even on their first day. A friend recalls that she was sent to the kitchen for 'elbow grease'. Nearly everyone who entered Goldenbridge was tricked into going to the kitchen for elbow grease. This was the way we learned, from day one, that elbows should move so that they worked efficiently. No gentle wiping of surfaces; everything required strong elbow grease. When my friend arrived at the kitchen, she met a staff member who took her to the 'kitchener', an industrial-sized cooking pot, full of boiling water. The woman dunked the child's elbow in it and laughed as she told her, 'That's elbow grease.' A scalded and angry girl left the kitchen to rejoin the rest of us, having endured her ritualistic welcome.

We suffered pain and grief like everybody else when our relatives died. My favourite aunt was very ill for a long time, with a rare heart condition. Though I hardly ever saw her after we went to Goldenbridge, I still loved her very much. I remember my mother taking us to see her when she was brought to hospital in Dublin. Dr Barnard, the famous heart surgeon, saw her, but it was too late and she died soon afterwards. She wanted a pair of rosary beads that I'd made and I got a set, though not made by me, from Goldenbridge to put in her coffin. I don't know if the beads ended up in her coffin, but I felt guilty for years afterwards because I hadn't personally made them for her.

When first cousins of mine arrived in Goldenbridge, I was shocked and confused because I never expected that to happen. I recall talking to them and finding out that they were only coming in for a short time while my aunt, their mother, was in hospital. I felt envious of them for this but was also concerned about how they would cope. Curiously, I also experienced them as encroaching on our territory. It was not so much the physical territory of Goldenbridge, because I had no attachment to that. It was much more that they had become part of what, up to now, belonged to our branch of the family – the shame of being there. I felt that acutely. My cousins, lucky for them, left within weeks. I remember feeling relieved when other children said they were only staying while their mother was having another baby. I used to think they were lucky because they didn't have to suffer for long. Sometimes, though, things didn't turn out as expected, and they too had to stay until they were 16.

We were among the lucky few who, as siblings, could stay together. We were lucky too, in that both our parents came to visit. In the beginning, my father visited on a Wednesday while my mother visited on a Sunday. My father used to sit us in the back of his car, much like the night before our arrival in Goldenbridge, while he sat alone in the front. He hardly looked at us or spoke to us as we ate the crisps and silvermints which he brought us. When we finished eating them, he led us back to the front porch where he said goodbye. He never hugged or kissed us on these occasions. Still, we were delighted that he came to visit, and it indicated that he showed some interest in us, for a while.

Our mother came every Sunday and always took us out for the afternoon. Quite often she brought new clothes with her and we would change into them before going out. Presumably she did this so that we wouldn't look like orphans. She always took us to see our relatives.

I always enjoyed my aunt's cooking on those visits, especially on my confirmation day when she made a feast of dumplings. I filled my stomach like it hadn't been filled since I had entered Goldenbridge! On birthdays my mother brought us birthday cakes, and she always remembered our birthdays, unlike my father.

On the way back to Goldenbridge she always took us to Mulvin's sweet shop in Inchicore village and allowed us to have whatever sweets or little toys we liked. She was particularly generous to my youngest brother Christopher and bought him expensive toys, especially when he cried because of going back to the orphanage.

I always thought that my mother felt guilty about leaving us and particularly about Christopher because he was still only a baby. She has since told us that every week she left us at Goldenbridge she cried all the way home and all through the night.

One day, in October 1964, I realised that I hadn't seen Christopher for some days. Naturally, I was really worried about him, and when my mother came on the following

Sunday, she told me he was in hospital, with ring-worm. This confused me, because we thought ring-worm came from cows and I knew he hadn't been near any. He stayed in hospital for 10 weeks, during which time I didn't see him. I dread to think what was going on in his little mind, when he found himself separated from us for such a long period of time.

In November of the same year I noticed that I hadn't seen my twin, Michael, for some days. Once again, I was really worried and for some reason this time I hesitated to tell my mother. It might have had something to do with the fact that I felt responsible for my brothers. I thought it was my job to mind them and know where they were. Recalling those times, even now, instantly evokes deep worry. In any event, I had to inform her and it was only then that she told me he was with her in my aunt's house. I was upset but very relieved. Adults had a strange habit of witholding information which left children confused and upset.

It was policy to transfer boys, when they were 10 years old, from Goldenbridge to the Christian Brothers in Artane. My mother was informed by a nun that Michael was going to Artane. A father of a number of children in Goldenbridge met my mother during visiting time and became quite friendly with her. One of his boys had been transferred to Artane and this man advised my mother not to allow her sons to go there. He had strong feelings about that. I recall that he once invited all of us to his home in Dominick Street to discuss the matter. We did visit, but at the time I didn't connect their discussions with the loss of my twin brother.

My mother wrote to the Department of Education, Industrial Schools section, and sought permission to take Michael home. This was agreed to and for some reason, unknown to me, shortly afterwards Michael was moved to St Saviour's Boys' Home, in Dominick Street, run by the Dominican order of priests. In the light of all we have since heard about Artane, I think he and my other brothers had a very lucky escape. Nine months later, my younger brother disappeared, and again nobody bothered to tell me. This time, though, I realised that he had been transferred. Just days before his tenth birthday, my mother sought to have him transferred to St Saviour's Boys' Home. This had been agreed to by the Department of Education.

The cruelty of not informing us of the whereabouts of our siblings was in my case mild, compared with others. For example, a good friend of mine had a twin sister. Aged 12, they had lived in Goldenbridge together all their lives. The day one of the nuns was transferred from Goldenbridge to work in St Kieran's Boys' Home in Rathdrum, she hand-picked eight girls to go to work for her, without payment. They worked there for many years. My friend's twin was one of them.

These girls had been removed in the middle of their education. This seems to have been a common practice in institutions at this time. In those days young girls working in homes were often not paid, often not actually regarded as employees, which meant that social insurance or salaries were not paid. These arrangements also split up families. This, I think, was downright cruel. What was even worse, no one bothered to tell their siblings or their friends who were left behind.

The case of the twins was particularly sad. I can only begin to imagine what is must have felt like for them to be so suddenly separated from each other. They had no contact with their parents and there were no other family members in Goldenbridge. They were completely bereft on being separated because they had been very close. For two years my friend heard nothing of her sister. Then, one summer's day, while we were in St Joseph's, the Goldenbridge holiday home which was also in Rathdrum, they met each other, quite by chance, on the street. It amazes me that the nuns in Goldenbridge made no attempt to facilitate a meeting between them, even though my friend had spent all of the previous summer in Rathdrum not knowing her sister was in the same town.

The Black Doll and the Swing

My mother was materially very generous to us, so we never lacked sweets or toys, when we were with her. She bought us lots of clothes, as well as giving us money. One winter's day in January 1964, she brought me a beautiful black doll and I was delighted with her. But ultimately the doll became something of a burden to me. This was because I had nowhere safe to keep her and it was impossible for me to carry her around.

A black doll was a very unusual thing in Ireland. I was rather proud to have one, and worried about what to do with her. In the end, I settled for taking the risk of leaving her in my bed. At times such as this, I was amazed at how impractical my mother could be, but it is indicative of the fact that she had no idea of the way we lived, now that we were in Goldenbridge.

Having left my doll in the bed, I went through the usual routine of the morning and after lunch time duties went out to the yard as usual, to play. To my horror, I saw my lovely black doll on the roof. She hadn't a stitch of clothing left on her and she looked totally abandoned, just thrown on the roof of St Brigid's corridor.

This roof was slated and sloped into the yard, so it was temptingly close to me. I had a notion that all I had to do was run from one side of the yard to the other, jump, and my doll would be rescued. But I didn't allow for the fact that there was a row of swings, and that they were in motion. One hit me and threw me firmly to the ground. My left eye was split open and I bled profusely. Two staff members arrived on the scene, gave me a wad of cotton wool and took me to Dr Steeven's Hospital. On the journey I was sore, shocked and frightened that I might lose my eye. I've no idea whether or not I was kept in and I never saw my black doll again.

The event did serious damage to my left eye, and for years after I had to attend the Eye and Ear Hospital for treatment. This included undergoing an operation for a squint which developed as a result of the accident. A staff member brought me for the operation, by bus. We were taken to a ward where a nurse immediately cut my hair. I was upset by this and then the staff member left and I was alone with my little bag containing a nightdress and a washbag. I was put to bed and I can still recall the layout of that ward and the position of my bed, just under a high window. Later, the nurse said I'd have to have a bath. This made me anxious as I was visualising how baths were in Goldenbridge. To my surprise, this was nothing like I'd expected because the nurse was gentle and caring.

I had my operation the next day and when I came to I got a fright, because my eyes were covered and I couldn't see. Eventually the nurse removed the plaster and my eye was quite sore. I remember rushing to the bathroom with a nurse and she was happy for me. Still I was frightened out of my wits because my eye was very red and I thought it would never get better.

The other people in the ward were all women and some of them were kind to me. Their visitors brought me in sweets and fruit and I liked that, but I felt very much like 'the orphan'. They knew I didn't have visitors and I thought that I stuck out like a sore thumb. I was ashamed and embarrassed about it and wondered why my mother didn't come to visit. After a while, I couldn't stick the shame anymore and when the visitors came, turned my head away, and pretended to be asleep. They kindly continued to leave me sweets, but I didn't have to face them anymore.

Sundays were a different matter though. I felt more hopeful and leaned on the window sill watching visitors coming and going, and fully expecting to see my mother and brothers. For the first few Sundays I was hurt and confused when they didn't come. After that it became increasingly more painful and I was angry with myself for continuing to wish they would come. I never allowed my distress to be seen but I was a mass of uncried tears, and felt I was dying inside. I came to the conclusion that my mother didn't love me or care about me, and I felt utterly abandoned. All the Sundays I waited for her, I pictured her going to Goldenbridge to collect my brothers and then coming to see me. I was even more upset when on my return to Goldenbridge they confirmed she had taken them out every Sunday, as usual. It dawned on me, not for the first time, that my mother preferred my brothers to me.

This was shown when Michael, my twin, was in Cherry Orchard Hospital. She rightly took the rest of us from Goldenbridge to see him, even though none of us was allowed into his room. We waved at him through the window outside, and my mother threw him kisses. I recollect also that when Christopher was again in Dr Steeven's Hospital, this time as a result of having broken his leg in Goldenbridge, she took us to see him every Sunday. That was perfectly appropriate, and I was happy, indeed very happy, to see them. But it was clear to me that I was not worth the same effort. I thought seriously about these things and I was very sensitive to such hurts. I know in retrospect that, generous as my mother was, this episode deeply affected my relationship with her.

Bad eyesight caused serious problems for me at school. A formidable inspector from the Department of Education used to come to check our knitting and sewing. This woman took her task seriously and she went around to every child, and told us of the importance of being able to sew and knit. She took samples of our work away with her, because they were so good, though mine was the exception which she took away because it was so bad. She used to say to me, 'You could drive a horse and cart through those stitches.' Like all the adults in Goldenbridge, she criticised me because of something that was outside of my control. The fact was I couldn't sew simply because I couldn't see and she probably didn't even know this.

The White Doll

Soon after the saga with my black doll, my mother bought me a smaller white one. My white doll looked cute in her lovely fine cotton quilted bed with pretty flowers. On the bus going back to Goldenbridge, I held her close, admired her and made her comfortable, as a mother would a tiny baby.

When we got off the bus, to my horror I found myself standing on the pavement without my doll. I was so distraught! I cried, fretted and pined for her. My mother promised she would call to CIÉ lost property office to see if she had been handed in. I thought about her all week and when my mother came on Sunday, without her, I sensed that she had forgotten her. My mother said she had tried to find her but hadn't succeeded. I continued to live in hope and, for many Sundays after, pestered her about my doll. Eventually I gave up asking, because I realised that she hadn't actually looked for her at all.

In retrospect, I think that the loss of these dolls encapsulates all the many losses I experienced throughout this period of my life. It continues to affect me to the present day, in that, when I lose small personal items, I feel unreasonably sad and it takes me a long time to regain my equilibrium.

Fights and Squabbles

In the orphanage you had to be able to fight and when you were small, in order to survive, you had to have someone to protect you. It was not only the nuns and staff who beat you. Bigger boys and girls also beat and bullied you. Early on, my mother recruited a protector for us, an older, stronger girl. I don't know the circumstances of how she made this arrangement, but my mother paid this girl to protect us. This is the one area of our lives in Goldenbridge to which my mother was sensitive, and it went some way towards easing the burden of living there. This girl would prevent others from hitting us and warn them off, beating them off if necessary. We were lucky that my mother was in a financial position to do this, because there was a definite hierarchical system and big girls were much stronger than us little ones.

All the same, I began to work hard at developing my own physical strength, because when I first went to Goldenbridge I quickly learned that my survival depended upon it, as did that of my brothers whom I protected. Other boys bullied and pushed them around and while they may have thought it was fun, I could see that my brothers were distressed by it. I hated to see them suffer, and I determined to stop it if I could. In the beginning I could do nothing but observe and empathise with them, but gradually it wore me down and I became tense and angry. I could literally feel my blood boil with hurt, pain and rage.

One day the other boys were boxing my brothers in a corner of the Rec. Suddenly I flipped and ran to find a sweeping brush. I lashed out at them until I was exhausted. I was terribly upset over the incident, not least because I feared the consequences. As it transpired, nothing happened and the boys stopped picking on my brothers.

One girl bullied me for a number of years. It all began when the nuns decided to divide the Sacred Heart dormitory into four separate units. As a result there was limited sleeping space, and they decided to have us sleep two to a bed. Another girl and I were to share a bed. From the first night it was hell. This girl pushed me almost out of the bed as I tried to sleep. I was terrified to move, because she constantly punched me and told me to 'shut up breathing'. This went on, night after night, until I was literally afraid to breathe, such was my fear of her. I held my breath for as long as I could, before I dared to release it. It was a crazy situation, but very real, nevertheless.

When we went to Rathdrum on holidays she used to take me into the toilet, in the main building, when the nuns and staff were gone to bed. Once inside, with the door secured, she would begin her ritual, a foolish children's game but confusing and upsetting to me. She sat on the toilet and I had to stand with my back to the door. Then she acted out the role of someone putting on a peaky cap while saying out loud, 'Peaky cap, peaky cap.' She always laughed and I had to pretend it was funny too and laugh with her. For me it was intimidating, and my mind was fully occupied with the thought and the fear that I could be caught in a toilet with another girl. A very serious offence indeed. She, however, didn't seem in the least concerned about this.

A relative of this girl was extremely good to her and always brought her lots of sweets. This presented her with a problem: if she admitted possessing sweets, she ran the risk of having them confiscated. To avoid this she hid them in the visitors' room, 'the villa', which was a separate building. To have been caught retrieving her sweets would have brought down on her the most terrible punishment. Her solution was simple – to bully me into going to the villa, in the pitch dark, to get them for her.

One day I had had enough of being bullied and decided to fight back. I, and several girls I had confided in, had to dry cutlery outside St Brigid's which was then used as a dining room. As we worked, I trembled with fear about my proposed plan of action. I awaited an opportunity to launch the defence of my sanity, and didn't want the day to pass without doing so. My tormentor didn't disappoint me. As predicted, she made a snide remark to me as she passed by me. Taking her completely by surprise, I jumped on her, and beat her good and proper. All my pent-up rage and frustration poured out of my fist, and I wouldn't stop until I felt that she had got the message, loud and clear, never to mess with me again. That was the end of her bullying me and I was free to breathe again.

Sometimes victory was not necessary. The willingness to get into a fight was often enough to win respect. It happened to me when I challenged another big girl and took a beating for it. The incident occurred in the dining room where both of us were assigned to clear the dishes and wash the tables. She came to me and demanded my cloth, and I refused to hand it over. Even though she bashed me, I gained some satisfaction in that I managed to hold on to the cloth with all my might. Word spread, and after that the big girls left me alone.

Such was the rhythm of life in Goldenbridge that only the fittest survived the hierarchical system and the petty violence among the children, violence they had learned from the systematic abuse that was so palpable and which permeated the atmosphere of the orphanage at all times.

CHAPTER FIVE

– Playtime Horrors –

In the early weeks of the summer months, during which we were free from making rosary beads, we could play in the yard on warm days. We still had to do all our other work first, but we got several hours playtime between meals. It was great fun and we really savoured those times. We'd have time to break into groups of friends. We played all the normal children's games of hopscotch, skipping, rounders, but I'd speculate that we must have been the most skilled ball players in the country.

Skipping was something we also enjoyed immensely and involved larger groups playing together. Each taking a turn on the ropes, those of us skipping would sing, 'Silk, satin, cotton, rags'. Whichever of these words we were knocked out on would denote the material we were going to wear on our wedding day. Needless to say, we got upset if we fell on the word 'rags'. Some of these games were very fast and the rope-turner would often end up on her back. One of the fastest skipping games involved the girls turning the ropes as fast as they could, while one of us skipped to the words 'High, low, slow, medium, hockey, rockey, pepper'. I can still hear the sound of the rope as it whished off the ground.

While many of us participated and enjoyed ourselves at these times, others were unable to do so for various reasons. It was not uncommon to see children sitting on the ground, thumb in mouth, rocking backwards and forwards, sometimes literally falling asleep. In fact, several girls recollect that I was one such child. While I don't remember that, I recall others doing it. It was not a pretty sight to see, though. It wasn't nice either, on cold days, when we had neither cardigans nor socks. We sat huddled together for warmth, saying to each other, 'I'm freezing. Are you? Feel my hands.'

Squabbles are normal among children. In Goldenbridge though, they were often caused by what we perceived to be disloyalty. In retrospect, I can see that much of the betrayal and disloyalty was caused by the attitude of the staff and nuns. They didn't take kindly to groups of friends forming what they called cliques, and they actively participated in breaking them down. Like all children, we had preferences about who we liked to spend time with, and often we had squabbles about who should play in our group. A girl I liked a lot was often left out of groups, and some of my friends used to tell her to go away, that they didn't want to play with her. I always hated to see that and I was forever taking her by the hand and bringing her into the group, telling them that I wouldn't play with them if she couldn't. It always worked, so cliques weren't always the bad things that the nuns made them out to be.

Nevertheless, the nuns and staff actively discouraged us from maintaining the nuances of childhood friendships, and stopped us whispering to each other or having secrets among ourselves. They beat us into revealing to them, in front of everybody, what a friend had told us privately. This created an atmosphere of suspicion, mistrust and fear of friendships. As a result, relationships were often fickle and superficial.

As in so many things, there were some exceptions to the rules, and I recall two girls who were friends throughout their time in Goldenbridge. In their case, a member of the staff liked them and tolerated their friendship, even teasing them by calling them 'the love birds', though one of the nuns, I recollect, did all in her power to break their bond.

Occasionally, poignant incidents occurred while we

played in the yard. A friend distinctly remembers that a big girl came up to her one day and said, 'You're eight today.' Her first thought, apart from the surprise of discovering she had a birth date, was: 'Double my age and I'll be out of here.' Another girl recalls that a teacher called her in from the yard one day, telling her, 'There's a woman in the porch hall to see you.' The girl went there to find a woman she didn't know offering her a bar of chocolate. The woman didn't say who she was, and the child didn't ask. Some years later when this girl was in hospital, the same woman, without as much as approaching her bed or greeting her, threw her a bag of sweets from the door and left. To this day, she has no idea who the woman was, though she speculates that she must have been a relative of hers.

In the yard we also had to defend ourselves against Jenny, the monkey, which would be let out of the cage to run amok amongst us. But we would be thrashed if we defended ourselves. There was also a dog, an alsation, who ran wild too. We children were terrified and no doubt so was the dog. He'd chase us, and if we ran frightened, he'd snap at us, and we would get the blame. Those supervising the yard simply couldn't or wouldn't see things from our perspective. They couldn't identify with the world of children and see that we were obviously terrified.

The 'Rec'

The Rec was a very large room, with a stage at the top which was used for Christmas plays and storage space. It was a plain room with a large wooden bench around the walls. Gas heaters, ceramic-framed with pulleys which were too high for us to reach, heated the room. When we got the chance we stood on the bench and reached up with our hands to feel the warmth. Otherwise, these heaters were useless. The top walls were a dirty cream colour while under the bench was painted blood red.

Occasionally when we played in it illegally, such as the day we organised an impromptu game of rounders, we got into serious trouble. During this game, I managed to hit a window, and worse still, smash it. A nun came on the scene and she told me I would have to stay in Goldenbridge until I paid the costs of replacing the window. I was about 11 years of age at the time, and I tried frantically to calculate how long this might take. I really believed she had the power to do this and I felt miserable about it. In time, though, she stopped talking about it and I never played rounders after that.

The toilets were an important feature in the Rec, not least for the practical purposes they served. They were very low on the ground, the only toilets suitable in height for small children. They were incredibly dirty, despite the fact that they were cleaned every day. The walls were partially covered in faeces, the floor soaking wet with the remains of toilets which were forever flooding. Longer than average chains were regularly broken or missing. Some of the children used the chains in their attempts to emulate the priests who shook the thurible – an incense container, held on long chains, at Benediction. It's a pity they weren't able to infuse the toilets with the same lovely aroma of the incense.

The Rec was used for activities such as old time waltzing. Couples from outside, presumably local people, used to come on a Monday night, to be taught to dance. I recall being in the Rec with them but I'm unsure about whether or not we were there to learn or to watch. Two other gentlemen, who also taught us Irish dancing, used it on Wednesday nights. One of them, a stout, silver-haired, neat man, was always impeccably dressed and wore the shiniest black shoes for dancing. He taught us reels, jigs and hornpipes, line by line. The longest line was that described as 'the lazy line' – those of us who didn't bother to make an effort – and the dancing teacher would teach us by repeating over and over again, as he became redder in the face, '1,2,3,4,5,6,7, lift those feet well off the floor; 1,2,3,4,5,6,7, lift those feel right up to heaven.' For some reason, the nuns and senior staff nearly always attended these classes with us, though the various dancing teachers over the years were perfectly capable of containing us themselves. I remember that while these teachers were firm but nice with us, some of the nuns used to come behind us and poke and hit us with sticks as we danced, to encourage us to be more active. This didn't endear us to Irish dancing, particularly when we got older and thought it was unfashionable. A number of the girls were particularly good at it and some of us, including myself, were known to win an occasional medal at the annual *feis* held in the Mansion House.

We used to do 'drill', physical exercise, in the early days. This involved marching up and down the Rec like soldiers, as well as racing, leap frogging and jumping over stools. We wore a uniform of a white t-shirt and blue shorts. We did strenuous exercise to rhymes with ever increasing speed.

We played table tennis for a short while too and we really enjoyed it. A teacher was employed for this and I don't know why it suddenly stopped. Perhaps it was because we created a lot of noise during tennis, the worst being the sound of the tables crashing to the floor as we rushed to get the ball over the net.

Drama lessons were introduced when I was about 11 years old. At that age, we were becoming ever more conscious of our appearance and the drama teachers decided to put on *Playday in Happy Holland*. They were both nice to us but one, whom we considered old because of her grey hair and her 'hush puppy' type boots, became exasperated with us very quickly. The younger one, who was extremely thin and had very fine hair, helped keep us under control. We played tricks on them, such as hiding their gloves. They would be in a right state when it was time to go home and they couldn't be found. We always returned them but not before they had almost lost their patience with us.

For the play we dressed up in Dutch clothes, right down to the clogs. The best part for us was that we got to wear wigs of long hair with plaits. We hated taking them off because we had to go back to our own short-back-and-sides haircuts.

The nuns from the convent came to watch the films with us in the Rec. They sat at the back, on nice cushioned seats, while we sat on hard wooden ones. Then all windows were covered in what seemed like the same black material as the nuns' habits. We watched films with mostly religious themes, especially on Christmas Day. The projector regularly broke down or the reels of film snapped. Still, the nuns always managed to get them working in the end. *The Greatest Story Ever Told* was a favourite as was *The Story of Bernadette* and *The Sound of Music*. The nuns laughed heartily at *Old Mother Reilly* films, some of which we didn't understand. We did, however, laugh heartily ourselves while watching *The Girls of St Trinian's*, and Laurel and Hardy films.

We were treated to occasional concerts by well-known Irish performers. The Clancy Brothers came once and rumour spread that one of them was a brother of one of the nuns. Whether or not it was true, the rumour was very active. Dickie Rock also came once as did the 'All Priests Show'. Actors from the famous RTÉ radio programme, 'The Kennedys of Castleross', came to visit us. They arrived with a huge box of chocolates which they had apparently bought themselves because a chocolate company would not donate them. When they left, one of the nuns wanted to know which of us had written inviting them to visit. It was never established whether anyone had in fact, but some girls got a beating for it anyway.

Another function of the Rec was its occasional use as a dormitory when the Sacred Heart dormitory was being redecorated, and when refugees came to stay. I recall having the best sleep of my stay in Goldenbridge there when I was 8 years old. I attribute this to the fact that we were left unsupervised for most of the night, and so felt more relaxed going to sleep.

Playtime on Wet Days

But my strongest memories of the Rec centre around its use at so-called 'recreation time' on wet days. I came to associate it with scenes reminiscent of houses of horror. You need to hit a child awfully hard to leave the mark of a hand on his or her face. You have to hit a child even harder to burst an eardrum. All of this we experienced in the Rec. It's true that most of the physical marks have faded from our faces now but many adults who were raised in Goldenbridge are walking around today with damaged hearing from being punched in the Rec. I have a friend who still suffers days of excruciating headaches from having been repeatedly punched on the ear when she was there. It's important to remember that it was not only the nuns who were cruel. Some of the worst violence was done by young female staff members.

When the nuns went for their meals and left the staff in charge, it was as if their collective aggression was suddenly unleashed and inflicted on us. Whether it was that the Rec was the most distant room from the front porch, or that the staff felt they couldn't cope with the noise level of so many young children, it was here that they unleashed their real demons.

Whatever the explanation, here we sat, boys and girls, on the long hard wooden bench, legs dangling because we were so small. We were ordered by the staff to put our fingers tight on our lips and to remain in that position, staying absolutely silent for the entire recreation period.

The staff stood with their backs to the stage but facing us, waiting for an unfortunate child to fidget, whisper, or look sideways. Of course, children could not realistically be expected to sit like statues for such long periods. One child would look at the child beside her, or whisper, or look at a friend across the room. At once one or two women would dash down from their positions at the front of the stage. They dived on the children concerned, pulled them off the bench, usually by the hair, and beat them with all their might around the room. Children would be left with bald patches and a stinging sensation in their head from having had their hair pulled from the roots. We would be cowering and covering our legs to protect ourselves from the blows raining down on us. If we could get to a corner we faced one side of our bodies towards the wall, in order to protect at least half of us. With hands protecting our heads, blows would land on our wrists, hands and arms. I can still feel the pain on the bone of my wrist as I recall these beatings.

Often, in the process, we were literally stripped naked as staff tore off our clothes in the process of pulling us around. They scratched us and battered us till we were black and blue. Then they threw us to the floor. When we were down, they kicked us. Children would be left sprawled out on the floor and then would be grabbed by the hair and pulled to a standing position. I can still see children unable to stand, and falling to their knees. It was a terrifying spectacle to observe these frenzied attacks on small children which seemed to go on for a very long time. Usually three or four children were thrashed during these sessions. It seemed to go on for the whole hour, with no respite. When one staff member's energy was spent, another would take over. They were scenes reminiscent of concentration camps and indeed we often ascribed this term to Goldenbridge. The wonder is that these people didn't actually kill us. I often feared for my life and the lives of others in the Rec and elsewhere.

The question no doubt arises: What did other adults do while this orgy was in progress? Those women who were not taking part in the assault stood by and looked on, as if nothing out of the ordinary was happening. I never knew any of them to intervene to stop the savagery which their co-workers were inflicting on us. Cruelty has many faces, and indifference is one of them.

We children continued to sit on our benches with our fingers tight on our lips, terrified to move, attempting to maintain silence. Most looked shell-shocked, some literally shaking like leaves. Many cried, while some wet their underwear with sheer fright. Children who suffered physical disabilities were not spared and it was particularly harrowing to see them, even more defenceless than we were, being subjected to such terror. The nuns seemed to have difficulty accepting physical disabilities of any kind and commonly tried to force children with polio, for example, to stand straight and walk as if they hadn't such a disability.

I shall never forget the fear that was induced in me when I saw staff rushing in my direction to grab a child. The sheer relief I felt when it wasn't me was short-lived while my attention simultaneously turned towards feeling abject sorrow for the child who was now receiving such a terrible thrashing. This violence affected us so much that it registered on some of our faces. I remember one girl who spent all of her recreation time standing with her back to a wall, a blank look on her face, refusing to take part in anything. Her expressionless face still haunts my memory.

I had very strong feelings and reactions to what I was witnessing and experiencing. I thought it was disgusting and that the staff were completely mad. I seethed with rage but was also very frightened. I lived in constant dread of these orgies of violence being unleashed on me.

At the time, though, determination not to be broken by these people was uppermost in my mind. I consoled myself with the thought that one day I'd be strong enough to do something about it, whether it was inside or outside of

Goldenbridge. I had no idea how I would do that, but at the time all I wanted was to be physically stronger and unafraid of them. My mind ran riot thinking about things I would do, if I had the power. I desperately wanted them to experience the hurt and fear and terror that they induced in us.

As it transpired, their violence affected me deeply and for over 20 years I couldn't get the sights of beatings, burst eardrums and snotty noses out of my mind. I also experienced constant flashbacks to scenes and sounds of children screaming, crying, sobbing, and experiencing panic attacks.

In retrospect, I think that the 'Rec' in Goldenbridge was appropriately named, since we were left well and truly 'wrecked' by the end of so-called recreation.

CHAPTER SIX

– Holy Terrors –

The convent at Goldenbridge was home to about 30 nuns, ranging in age from early twenties to late seventies. Only a few of them worked in the orphanage. About half of the community were known to us on sight. We would see them walking around, with heads bent, looking suitably pious, reading from a black, leather-covered book, their 'breviary'. We would also see them at occasional films in the orphanage. They all looked pretty much the same to us, all in black, dismal-looking habits and black veils. Under the veils they wore a white wimple on the forehead and around the face, and across the chest a heavily starched linen bib known as a gamp.

Those we did meet rarely spoke to us, and we didn't know their names. They knelt less than 3 feet behind us for all religious services in the chapel, and they could have come out to greet us, unless of course they weren't allowed to. The only exception to this was when some of us would be sent to clean the church or to pick apples in the orchard for the nuns.

Those of us who attended the secondary school obviously knew the nuns who taught there. For the majority of children in the orphanage, however, there was no access to the nuns in the convent. As a child, I was aware and conscious of this lack of contact, and I wondered about it as I got older. When we at the secondary school talked to the others in the orphanage about nuns in the school, we might as well have been referring to nuns who lived on another planet. They didn't know who we were talking about.

In retrospect, I formed the opinion that there was a policy of complete separateness at Goldenbridge. Between the orphanage and the convent was a gate, known as 'the wicket' – but christened 'the wicked' by us – which, when locked at night, firmly separated the two worlds. In their behaviour towards us, the nuns conveyed the attitude that those in the convent were 'all good' and should not be contaminated by us bad entities. We weren't worthy of interaction with them. Contact with us children was for lesser mortals, and that seemed to include the few nuns appointed to run the orphanage. There was, even then, a strong hierarchical and discriminatory system operating within the convent. I remember, for example, sensing that the nuns who worked in the convent kitchens, one in particular who worked with the poor and who was a genuine example of mercy, were considered lesser people than the educated nuns who taught in the school.

A reverend mother was responsible for the running of the convent. I knew nothing about them. I recall seeing one of them on the grounds of the convent, but I've no recollection of her ever visiting us in the orphanage in her capacity as reverend mother, even to say hello to the children. I know that it was the reverend mother, not the nuns in charge of the orphanage, who signed the papers admitting and discharging my brothers and myself from Goldenbridge orphanage. This would seem to indicate that these were the individuals who held ultimate responsibility for the orphanage. If this is so, it is frightening and shocking to reflect on the lack of interest they displayed in it and in the children for whom they were acting as legal and moral guardians.

The nuns working in the orphanage in my time there included one little old nun whom I only vaguely remember. She used to sit in the workroom with a staff member, working hard from morning till night, sewing and mending our clothes. I don't recall her ever speaking to us, but she did not engage in cruelty of any kind. How she tolerated working in an airless room, full of clothes from floor to ceiling, is beyond me. No doubt she was well and truly living out her vocation, silently and without complaint. She's the only nun to my knowledge who worked in the orphanage but slept in the convent.

One nun took charge of the babies' room, known as 'Guardian Angels', and she meted out humiliations by holding up our soiled underwear, on a stick, in the workroom. Some 'experts' on child-care policies of that era like to tell us that such was common practice in orphanages all over Ireland at the time, as if it in some way excuses this barbaric and humiliating activity. However, this knowledge goes no way towards easing the shame, the pain, the damage or the burden of this ritual, which we carried every week of our lives. It grieves and pains me even more to know that other innocent children were being subjected to this appalling suffering.

The reality for us children was that merely being in the presence of some of the nuns was an overwhelming experience. One in particular could induce terror in us just by looking at us in a particular way. We experienced this as intensely frightening and threatening. It was like being confronted by an extremely overpowering bully.

I remember vividly one nun, who was a relatively young woman of forty, the same age as my own mother, who gave us children the impression of being huge. A friend who grew up with me in Goldenbridge describes her as being built like a tank. Her eyes, while full of life, were hooded, small and sharp. These gave her the appearance of a bird of prey, ready to pounce on any unsuspecting child. She clenched her teeth firmly, even while speaking, which gave the impression that she was muttering, rather than speaking. Along with most of the nuns she had a strong country accent; this always made it very difficult for us to understand their commands.

One nun's demeanour was always that of someone with

the world on her shoulders, and of being in a desperate hurry, with no time to listen. When she raced along the many corridors in Goldenbridge, the base of her habit flew in all directions, and her long wooden rosary beads rattled, as if in protest, trying to keep pace with her. Her long and well-worn leather cincture (strap, hanging from the belt), displayed its occasional shiny surface, as she left behind a cold draught and an unmistakable whoosh sound. When she met us, she never failed to ask us, 'And where do you think you are going?' In our fear and fright, while attempting to answer her, she would shout at us, 'Speak up, speak up. Come on, hurry up. I haven't all day.' When we answered, she would inevitably find fault with whatever we were doing and order us back to wherever suited her.

One nun seemed totally negative in all her dealings with us. She never smiled at us or uttered a kind word to us. She seemed to expect us children to react, behave and respond as if we were adults. This nun could also give us a good solid slap across the face. The sheer harshness of her assaults on us was extraordinary. When we saw her, we ran the other way. We were terrified of her and of the sound of her voice.

Mornings, after breakfast, were always an ordeal. The children who had wet their beds, many of whom had already been punished by a staff member, were made to go and stand in one of the classrooms. I shall never forget the images I hold from those sessions. A large circle of children, boys and girls of all ages, stood in a semi-circle around the edges of the room. A nun would arrive and begin her ritual from her position on the rostrum, which was about 18 inches from the floor, but seemed very much higher to us at the time. We children, shaking in terror, and overwhelmed with fear and shame, would quake as she began her tirade of abuse, calling us at the very least, dirty, filthy, and bad, as she shook a stick at us. It was inevitable that some of us were in for a severe battering. As she continued berating us, she would become red in the face. She seemed to us to work herself into a frenzy. Then, suddenly, she would literally jump off the rostrum and pounce on any child in the circle within her reach. We were terrified of becoming the object of her frustrations. Our terror was nearly worse than the actual experience of being beaten by her. We became paralysed with fright. We would hold our breath while this orgy of violence took place, never knowing from moment to moment if we would hear our own scream on our next out-breath, from the pain felt from the beating. It was a horrible experience to observe one's friends and fear one's family members becoming the focus of her beatings. It would have been kinder for her to have given everybody an equal battering and be done with it.

I recall standing there as a child of 7 and 8, thinking to myself: This is just crazy. What is the point? Children wet the bed when they are scared. They don't do it just to annoy the nuns and staff, or just for a laugh. I remember rationalising that if they thought beating children would stop them wetting the bed, how come the same children were standing in front of them every day? It clearly wasn't working. But of course, that wasn't what the issue was about at all. I see, in retrospect, that it was foolish of me to think so rationally. These assaults had nothing to do with rational policies. The issue was very much deeper than this. Lots of children in Ireland, especially in institutions, were treated in this irrational way. As I see it now it was about providing an opportunity for the religious who ran these orphanages to express their own angry frustrations. It was about finding all sorts of excuses to 'punish' us for daring to exist. Remember, we were the children of 'sinners', of incompetents who couldn't look after their own children, of social outcasts. We bore their shame, their sin. We 'deserved' to be punished.

One nun who worked in the orphanage didn't spend very much time with us. She seemed to be always off out in the car.

She left her aura behind, though, and she might as well have been there all the time, such was her impact on us. She had a class to teach, but was rarely available to teach, so her pupils were often sent off to work in the kitchen, scullery and elsewhere. When she was there, she was continually interrupted by men calling, presumably trying to sell their wares. The children liked that because it got her out of the way for another while. When she was about, she would never interact with us in a pleasant or playful way.

One nun was indescribably cruel to girls who had problems with menstruation, those who sweated excessively, and girls who were 'developing' at a faster rate than she would have liked. I recall her name-calling and humiliating them for their feminine qualities. She often told girls that their mothers were nothing but prostitutes and that they would 'turn out just like their mothers'. One of her common statements was to tell the children: 'You are worse than the soldiers who crucified Christ.'

I recall a teenage girl who suffered terribly for being born a girl. She developed at a young age, sweated profusely, and had severe menstrual problems. She used to go white as a sheet, shiver and shake, and looked ready to faint at any moment. She was obviously completely drained by having her period much more often than was normal. She was very ill, but she has no recollection of ever visiting a doctor. There was a statue of the Virgin Mary in the yard and the girl was so distressed that she thought she saw it move. One day she was crying and shaking as she stood at the base of the steps leading into the corridor. Young as I was at the time, I sensed she was having a nervous breakdown. One of the nuns stood there, calling her 'Evil Eyes' among other names, and continually beating her whilst telling her the devil was coming out of her. This girl has beautiful eyes, but to this day she cannot tolerate anybody saying so. She deliberately walks with her eyes cast down to avoid bringing attention to them.

Another girl recalls being punished for some misdemeanour. Her punishment was to walk around the yard, in the winter time, in her nightdress only, barefoot, no cardigan, coat, or any other covering, for a week. She recalls developing pneumonia and being hospitalised for several weeks. Such was the strange behaviour in the orphanage.

Night times were very stressful. We were beaten badly enough by the staff, but they often took the notion of sending us to the landing, outside the nuns' cells, to await further punishment. Though this was common, we dreaded it. We would stand on the cold lino, with nothing on our feet or arms, wearing only a short-sleeved nightdress. It was pitch dark and freezing cold. We would stand, shivering and shaking with fear, as it was inevitable that we would get a beating for being there. One resident captures the mood of it in this poem which she wrote spontaneously some years ago:

> When I was just a baby,
> I was put into a school
> My mother passed me over
> To people who were cruel.
>
> What is this place
> That felt so cold?
> They beat and beat you
> When you were bold.
>
> They put you in the furnace
> When you stole a slice of bread
> And left you on the landing
> With fear running round your head.
>
> It was very cold on the landing
> You wished you were in bed
> Then the light goes on – she's coming up
> You're feeling all the dread.

Her footsteps are getting closer
And you're shaking like a leaf
You hear a noise, what is it?
It's just your chattering teeth.

You see a big black shadow
And she says, you in trouble again?
Before you can even answer
You feel the terrible pain.

My hands they throbbed
As I sobbed and sobbed
As I went back to bed
I pulled the blankets over me
And remembered what she said.

'You're as bold as brass
And cheeky too,
I'll beat the devil,
out of you.'

As we heard footsteps coming up the stairs, we were overwhelmed with anxiety and stood pushing and shoving each
other so that we were not the first in line for a beating. We figured the nun would be at her strongest then and that her
strength would diminish as she went through us. She would go
through the motions of asking us why we were there. We
would respond: Miss so and so sent us. That was enough. She
rarely waited to hear why, or allowed us defend ourselves
against the 'charges' laid against us. She would send children
there herself and then forget why. We never took the risk of
not turning up, for fear she would remember. Then the battering began, with her shouting, 'I'll flog you.' This was followed
by the sounds of children screaming, obviously in pain. Children wet themselves with fear and that would drive her into an
absolute frenzy. She continued to hit them as she called them

all sorts of names and ordered them to clean it up. The scenes were horrific and are indelibly etched on my mind.

On rare occasions a child might stand on the landing alone. I recall this happening to me. I was very young at the time and I stood there for the entire night. I was terrified to go to bed but I knew I hadn't been seen. I slithered down the wall and sat on the landing for some time, but I was afraid to sleep in case I was found. In the morning one of the nuns came out of her cell and whether or not she realised what had happened, she simply told me to go and get dressed. Some years later, an older girl who had left Goldenbridge was at bingo and met my mother. She told her about my standing on the landing all night and my mother scolded her for not informing her earlier but there was no question of any of us telling such tales to our family or anybody else for that matter. We had truly taken on the culture of secrecy and were not about to risk life and limb by being so foolhardy. Besides, some of our families and people who took us out were forever remarking to us that the nuns were great for looking after us. We said absolutely nothing, but we had very different perceptions. Such was our life at that time, we couldn't win, whether we told or not.

When we woke up one morning we had no inkling that a great day had arrived. I was attending one of my regular visits to the Eye and Ear Hospital. On my return, having missed dinner, I went straight to the Rec. When I got there, I was shocked to see almost all of the children crying. I asked why and someone managed to tell me that a particular nun was leaving. I was absolutely delighted, and I couldn't understand why they were sobbing. Eventually, they told me they weren't crying because she was leaving, they were upset because some-one told them there would be no one to buy food, and that we would all starve to death! It was one of those childish myths that sometimes circulated like wildfire. I remember pondering on this and wondering if I too should be upset and crying. I came to the conclusion that I shouldn't. Besides, I wasn't the only one not upset. One of my best friends was as happy as I was at the news. She and I ran around the place, telling the others not to worry. I didn't believe we would die of starvation. Anything was better than this life, I reasoned.

The personalities of some nuns changed while they worked in Goldenbridge, and this always shocked and disappointed us children. I remember one whom we really liked who changed within a matter of months. It's as if the system got to her and turned her into a different person. Whether she was unhappy as a nun, or disliked working in the orphanage, I don't know. Suddenly her appearance changed dramatically – it was difficult to recognise her. And her personality changed beyond belief and as a result we grew to dislike her intensely.

One nun is credited with introducing physical education and she was also obsessive about cleanliness and tidiness. This caused us problems because we stored food and other precious things up our sleeves which put them out of shape. Socks were forever falling down around our ankles, and under our heels, because they were too big or too small. It didn't help that we used our shoes and socks as banks where we stored big brown pennies, which made walking painful and often extremely difficult. Ill-fitting clothes were common and caused us a lot of discomfort. My youngest brother, Christopher, remembers someone trying to force a red polo-neck jumper over his head, which caused his neck to lock. As a result he couldn't move his head for a week. This nun used to make us stand and stretch our arms upwards, so that she could examine our clothes for holes, under the arms or on the elbows of our cardigans. She would also check we had the right number of buttons.

One nun, it seemed to me, must have come back home from Africa. I had the idea for several reasons. Firstly, when she came to Goldenbridge we had been wearing mantillas or straw hats going to the church. We liked the hats, which originally had nice coloured ribbons on them and elastic which helped to hold them in place, under the chin. Though there were plenty of hats, she began making bonnets, ridiculous looking bonnets more suitable for babies to wear. We would be mortified walking to the church in them, all laughing at each other. I thought this was a little bit odd, to say the least, but she insisted we wear them.

Some of the adults in Goldenbridge had very unrealistic expectations about what young children could do. I recall standing in St Teresa's, which at the time was unused, apart from storing the boys' lockers. These lockers were completely unsuitable for small boys because they were at least 6 feet tall, and had only the base and a high shelf at about 5 feet. One day one of the nuns decided to examine the lockers. All the boys were there, and for some forgotten reason, so was I. Perhaps it was that I was minding them that day. One by one, the nun checked the lockers and she found fault with every one of them. She beat each of the boys, aged between 5 and 9. By the time she got through the first few, the others were very frightened and upset. All this, because their lockers were untidy. I couldn't make sense of this behaviour at all. Having said that, one of the bigger girls in that era recalls that the same nun was very good to her. She was the one and only nun to my knowledge who actually encouraged the children to be in touch with their siblings. She used to give the bigger girls the bus fare to go and visit their brothers in Artane, and they were very grateful for that.

There was another nun who stayed a very short time, and this type of short stay happened frequently. She was tall and good looking and was in her thirties. She wore her wimple very much higher on her head, and it was more square looking than those worn by the other nuns. She was kind to us. She used to play netball with us in the yard, and she was good fun. She died while we were still there. When nuns in the convent died, we used to form a guard of honour. We would stand in the cold in a line from the chapel to the graveyard, while the funeral went on behind the walls. This nun's death was an exception. Some of us were sent to her cell to see her laid out. For many of us it was the first time we had seen a corpse and it wasn't something we wanted to repeat.

I'll always remember the day we were told that a new nun was coming, that she was very nice, and that she would be very understanding. I was struck by the fact that we were being spoken to like this. Something new was in the air. Around that time another nun occasionally went off to do weekend courses to England, to learn about child care, and she would come back and mention this. Beyond that, she didn't discuss it, but we children talked about it and wondered what it might mean. We had the feeling that it was going to be good.

The new nun was very attractive-looking, even in a habit. Everybody liked her. She was nice, but firm. She was no walk-over. She was assigned to the younger children in the Guardian Angels room and their dining room, and she was kind to them. At that stage, less emphasis was put on the making of rosary beads and I recall relatively pleasant times working with her and and one of the staff in St Patrick's room, making rugs with bird and kingfisher patterns. We stuck holy pictures on to cards. We also packed 'lucky bags', which contained fizz pops. These we didn't dare rob, much as we were tempted. The fizz would have given us away. We behaved well and were 'good', especially for this new nun. But it wasn't easy to resist the lucky bags because we were often very hungry. Sometimes, when everyone thought we were securely in bed, we would sneak down to the scullery and stuff handfuls of dry cocoa into our mouths, in an effort to reduce our hunger pangs.

Things never seemed to improve much in Goldenbridge. The nuns and staff continued to beat the children. One teen-ager ran away because she could no longer tolerate seeing the babies being slapped for wetting the beds. She managed, with the help of relatives, to escape to England and was never brought back.

One nun began to slap teenagers she disliked and we began to think that she actually resented us growing up and moving out of Goldenbridge. This was not a feeling we had from other nuns. She became vindictive and would order our hair to be cut. She seemed to dislike some of the girls with the same intensity that other nuns and staff showed when they made someone their pet. She would single them out to do the most unpleasant tasks, such as cleaning toilets, indoor and outdoor. Some girls who were aware that this nun disliked them tried very hard to please her, but once she 'had her knife in you', it was impossible to remove it. One friend of mine got the brunt of it. She protested about it, but the nun's reaction was to beat the girl so badly that the poor child fainted.

At this time I had several 'run ins' with one of the nuns because of physical problems. She told me straight to my face that she disliked me intensely. I could handle that, but I found it much more difficult to deal with her deliberate acts of humiliation and shaming behaviour. I suffered badly with dental problems, including having an extra tooth growing in my gum, which caused me untold pain. In addition, I had gum problems. I had to attend the dentist on an almost weekly basis. This I absolutely hated. Every other week, the dentist would cut my gums so that I'd be in absolute agony with pain. Blood would ooze out of my mouth, night and day. I looked 'bloody' for years, and I developed a severe dose of halitosis. I was perfectly aware of it and was supposedly being treated with medication, which didn't work, with the result that my breath had an unpleasant odour. I felt helpless to do anything about it and I was thoroughly ashamed of it. I didn't need anyone informing me every morning, as we lined up to get washed, that my breath smelled badly and that I was disgusting. I found that unforgivable and degrading.

One nun started to learn to drive while we were on holiday in Rathdrum. One day, she arrived back as usual from her practice run and was about to stop the car at the entrance steps to the main building, when suddenly there was an enormous bang. She had crashed the car and it looked very damaged. While some of us stood in shock, others laughed nervously. She finally emerged from the car, white as a sheet. She began to cry but I wasn't too upset for her, once she wasn't seriously hurt.

The courses taken in England finally brought about positive changes, such as separate dining rooms for each age group. A nun or member of staff took each group. A problem arose with regard to who would take the teenagers – I was in this group now. One woman came to our group room, St Philomena's, and told us about the problem. She said, 'I don't want you and Sr ... doesn't want you, nobody wants you.' At the time, we acted with bravado and pretended we didn't care. The truth is we did. In the end, each of them took us for a while.

I remember a lovely young nun who only stayed for a very short time while another nun was hospitalised. This nun was the most beautiful person who ever graced the floors of Goldenbridge. She was very young, perhaps late teens or very early twenties. Her eyes lit up pleasantly at the sight of children and she was loving and kind to them, bending down to their level and asking their names and speaking gently to them. She played the guitar and in the early evenings she used to sing and play it, while the younger children gathered round her, ever eager to be near her. In all of her dealings with us she was forever respectful, sensitive and considerate. I never knew her to raise her voice to a child and still she could maintain absolute control. I never saw her raise her hand to slap or beat a child, and I'd be very surprised to learn that she had. I had the feeling that she came from a loving home and had close relationships with her family because she talked to us about them. She was very good with teenagers too and I recall that she used to invite them to her room and have chats with them. She was fair in all her dealings with us and she never showed favouritism. I might add that I hardly ever spoke to her. By that time I had completely shut down on adults and didn't trust them, but I did observe her closely and I knew that all of the children liked her. She was a gem, and she had to leave all too soon.

She taught us all a song to welcome the other nun back from hospital. We lined up in the front hall, singing: 'Céad míle fáilte, a hundred thousand welcomes.' I'm not sure how many of us meant that, but I know that we would prefer to have been singing it for the nice nun. Some of the girls were so fond of her that when they left Goldenbridge they visited her. She has since left the Mercy Order and we met for a few hours in recent years.

The atmosphere and practices at the orphanage depended largely on the personalities of the individuals who held power there and who didn't appear to be accountable to anybody. If they were, I saw no evidence of it. Neither the mother superior, who had overall responsibility for the orphanage, nor the Department of Education, despite detailed reports of bad conditions made by its inspectors, took any effective action to alleviate the suffering of the children.

We were at the mercy of whichever individuals turned up with their own individual psychology and personal history. The general attitude was one of punishment and of expelling whatever tendencies we might have inherited from our parents. After that we simply had to put up with whatever the particular nuns and staff foisted upon us. Eventually we came to distrust anything good because it could be taken away from us at a moment's notice, or with no notice at all. The little glimmers of kindness from the occasional decent nun or member of staff were swamped by the overwhelming general harshness and cruelty of Goldenbridge.

CHAPTER SEVEN

– All Things Bright and Beautiful –

Some of the bigger companies in Ireland, Guinness, CIÉ and Urneys Chocolates, took us out for Christmas parties and day trips. This gave us some welcome respite from our usual routine. We sang happily on the coaches as we travelled to and from the venues. Even though these were happy occasions, we sang some of the saddest songs imaginable. One in particular, which the nuns hated us to sing, was 'Two Little Orphans'. Perhaps the lyrics hit them hard, but whatever it was, we seemed oblivious to the painful parallels in our own lives.

On arrival at the parties, we were seated at long tables where we were served with masses of food and sweets. Staff of the companies donated their time and efforts for us, and they were very good with us, and to us. They would comfort the younger children who were sometimes frightened or distressed in strange environments. They played with them, carried them on their shoulders, sat them on their laps, and hugged them. They engaged in 'normal' interaction between adults and children. Though they were complete strangers to us, they never took the liberty of shouting at us, striking us or being unkind to us in any way. I used to marvel at their ability to encourage us to behave well, without resorting to violence. I used to feel especially sad at the end of these days when we had to separate from people who had been kind to us. We generally behaved very well, just as we did in Goldenbridge.

Santa Claus was the main feature on these outings and we'd get presents such as bath cubes and soap sets. We would carefully peek at the gifts, just to establish what they were. Our hosts were probably puzzled when we didn't tear the parcels asunder. We had good reason for carefully opening our presents. In our minds, we had already established who would receive our gifts. The most popular recipients were host families and our parents. We very rarely kept them for ourselves.

When Santa left the parties, we were entertained with music. There was always a master of ceremonies who actively encouraged us to sing until the party was over. On the return trip, tired, excited and happy, we'd hoarsely and wearily sing:

> Here we are again, as happy as could be,
> All good friends and jolly good company.
> We never mind the weather, we never mind the rain,
> As long as we're together, here we are again.

The day after one such party in the Gresham Hotel was a day never to be forgotten. We had a great time at the party, and we were extremely impressed with our surroundings. I recall a lovely carpeted, softly-lit cloakroom, next to equally exquisite toilet facilities. To say we had never seen anything like it would be a gross understatement. We were enthralled with the chandeliers and the opulence of the facilities. We couldn't be dragged away from them and we spent most of the time running in and around this comfortable setting, and washing our hands with the nice soap. Someone took photographs of us, but that wasn't unusual on such occasions. What was unusual, however, was to see the end product published in a national newspaper.

One late afternoon, when we were back to our usual routine of making rosary beads, one of the nuns came in with a copy of the day's paper. She was like thunder, seething with anger and humiliation. There, for the whole country to see, was a large photograph of some of us hanging out of the coat rail in, you've guessed, the ladies' cloakroom in the Gresham Hotel. We received a long lecture about how ashamed of us she felt, how the nation would think we had never seen toilets in our lives. She speculated about how upset the staff at the Gresham Hotel must have felt when we insisted on playing in these areas. We became increasingly deflated, as she focused on the particular children who could be identified in the photograph. Because some of these now infamous children were known bed-wetters, she set about humiliating them, as she focused on their bad habits and individual characteristics. She punished them by banning them from attending any more Christmas parties for that year. She further threatened that if such an event occurred again, she would not allow us to attend Christmas parties in the future. I don't recollect attending another party in the Gresham Hotel.

Every year, with hundreds of children from other orphanages, we attended a folk dancing performance in the Mansion House. A sad feature of this event was that, for some children, it was the only occasion in the year when they would get a glimpse of sisters and brothers in other orphanages around the country. I still feel incredibly sad when I recall these scenes – children waving to their siblings across the hall, and others bumping into them by coincidence as we entered or left the venue. Some would break away from their groups in an attempt to seek out their siblings, only to be disappointed by not finding them or by 'getting caught' and being returned to their own group.

We enjoyed the music and the colours of the costumes worn by dancers, mainly women, from all over the world. The Ukrainian dancing and the colours and costumes of the Indian dancers were especially beautiful and made real some of the places we had learned about in school. I was fascinated by the amount and colours of the bangles worn by the Indian dancers. I used to sit and quietly watch them and think to myself that I'd love to be them. Their world looked so bright and cheerful and they were doing something they seemed to enjoy. I used to actively wish each time we went, that, as if by magic, the Indian women would somehow know that I liked their bangles and that they might offer some to me. Even though I enjoyed the dancing, much of my attention would be focused on this and I always came away from the function feeling somewhat disappointed that my wishful thinking hadn't materialised. I was very aware, at the same time, that my wishes were unlikely to be granted, but that didn't stop me feeling hurt and upset. I must have overcome this hurt because for some years after I left Goldenbridge, I made a point of attending this annual event and continued to enjoy it.

I was very conscious of the dreariness and darkness of our existence at this time, and I guess I wanted and needed a more colourful life. The bright atmosphere in the Mansion House resonated with the joy and happiness I experienced on Saturday evenings when I lived at home with my parents. The 'rag and bone men' as they were called used to come to our street around tea time. I don't recollect exactly what their business was, but I know the men used to knock on the doors looking for items which people didn't want. My twin, Michael, recalls that the men would shout, 'toys for rags'. Whatever their business, I was completely enthralled by the dray horse which they decorated with red and white tassels, and ringing bells. The cart would be full of beautiful, brightly-coloured, fine materials that brought joy to my heart. As a very young child, I used to rush outside at the sound of the ringing bells and the clip-clop of the horse's hooves. I'd stand by the cart, feeling sorry for the horse, which seemed old and weary, with blinkered eyes, big hairy feet, standing with his laden cart behind him. I would pet him and make reassuring sounds, while he, with head bent forward, ignored my presence, and ate from his sack of oats. It was little enough to hold on to, but the need for colour and intimacy in my imagination was enormous. So few events in Goldenbridge fed that need.

Other celebratory days in Goldenbridge included first communion and confirmation days. I had made my first communion before going there, but I recall my confirmation day as a mixture of dread in case I didn't know the answer to the question asked of each child, and excitement at wearing new clothes and having my photograph taken. Life centred very much around the religious calendar and all major feastdays involved extra time in the chapel. On Mercy Day we got a slice of sponge cake – always dry as chalk because it had been left on the table hours before it was due to be eaten.

Our 'Ladies'

At one time Goldenbridge advertised in the newspapers requesting families to take us out. Many people responded and some of us went out on Sundays, weekends and holiday times. We always called these families our 'ladies', even though there was usually a husband and children as well. The nuns would shout: 'Your lady's here. Go and clean your face', and depending on who they were, we'd be either instantly happy or suitably miserable. We never conveyed such feelings to the nuns or staff and just went meekly with whoever came for us.

Some families have since told me that as far as they were aware, they were never screened. They simply gave their name, address and telephone number, if they had one, and were given a date on which to return us. These families were told nothing about us. They were simply told to contact the nuns if we were troublesome or bold, and that was it.

Sometimes we grew fond of our ladies, but sometimes they would suddenly stop coming for us. Nobody ever told us why, except on an occasion that the nuns might say to us, 'No wonder Mrs so and so won't take you out anymore.' That would hurt us really badly and we'd realise that our lady didn't like us as much as we liked her. Sometimes we liked them enough to wish they could adopt us. Often it worked the other way too. The families would become fond of us, would want to adopt, but would not be allowed to. A few children were very relieved when adoptions didn't happen, because sometimes we just didn't like the family concerned.

While most of us liked and some even loved our ladies, it would sometimes happen that other members of their families and friends would hurt and upset us, or family conflicts would arise. One such family, I recall, had a daughter who was the same age as me, and I had some notion that they wanted me to play with her. Their daughter became jealous, which I couldn't even begin to understand, but I was upset about it all the same. Then I heard the parents discuss and argue about it and they decided to return me to the orphanage, and that was the end of that.

Sometimes there were bigger problems than that, and many of us suffered routine sexual or other forms of abuse which we couldn't talk about with the nuns. We felt that we wouldn't be believed since we were always being told about how good these families were for taking us out. We also felt that we would be blamed and told that we must have encouraged them, and we felt we were left with no option but to say nothing to any adult about it. There was also the risk, as we got older, that if the nuns got to know that we had any knowledge or experience of sex we were likely to be sent to a Magdalen asylum, because they would think we were now in moral danger.

Even though some parents, including my own, visited weekly, they often were not in a position to have us stay out overnight, or for holidays, and this caused difficulties between them and our ladies, which we had to deal with. My brother Christopher found himself in a terrible dilemma on his communion day. Our mother and his lady came to take him out for the day. No one told them this was likely to happen, and Christopher remembers a nun or teacher asking him which of his mammies he wanted to go with. He chose his mother but felt very upset because he loved his lady and she began to cry.

I remember well the first of the many families who took me out. In fact, they took two of us, for our summer holidays. We really enjoyed ourselves, visiting their family, as well as playing out on the street in their brand new housing estate which I thought was at the end of the world. The neighbours' children played with us without prejudice and let us use their bicycles and scooters. I couldn't believe that they were so generous. I'd forgotten what it was like to be able to get around so quickly. I loved the sense of freedom, with all the space in the world to play.

A newly married couple with a baby, these people were always kind to us. One of the happiest memories I treasure from my childhood, was a day that others might describe as a horribly wet, rainy day. For some reason, I was alone with the woman as we walked along a street in Dún Laoghaire. Neither of us had rainwear on and suddenly the heavens opened. Holding my hand, the woman regularly bent down to me and apologised because I was getting so wet. What she didn't realise was that getting soaking wet was the least of my worries. I was the happiest child in the world because, young as I was, I felt absolutely contented, free of all my worries, as my hand was held with all the tenderness she could impart. I felt on top of the world and as safe as could be.

Like so many families in the early sixties, this family had a statue of the Child of Prague. It sat on the window-sill, directly behind the bed which my friend and I shared. One morning we were playing, and the next thing we knew the statue was smashed on the floor. We were sick with fear as we sat for ages discussing how we would deal with this catastrophe. Would we tell them? Who would we say broke it? Would we hide it, or say nothing? Eventually we decided to tell them straight since we realised we probably had nothing to fear. When we did tell them, neither of them made a fuss. What relief we felt! You see, the breaking of a statue in Goldenbridge was a very serious offence, with very serious consequences.

When this couple tried to take us out again at Christmas, the nuns told them that we had gone out with another family, and we lost contact with them. When I was 17, on my way to the boat in Dún Laoghaire, en route to my new life in London, I visited them briefly. And in January this year, feeling somewhat nervous, I decided to visit them. In the 37 years since we'd first met, I'd never forgotten them. We were so happy to meet again, and we shared memories from all those years ago. For instance, they reminded me that when visitors came to the house, I would insist that they would not walk on the floor, but instead on the carpet, in the middle, in case they would dirty the floor. They related that I used to tell them that my father was gone to England to build a big house and that he would come back for us. This was rubbish but no doubt it gave me some consolation at that time. They told me that, as we played, I talked of courts and judges and they didn't know what to make of this.

They have since told me that a friend of the family had recorded us singing 'Oh Liverpool Lou' and still has the recording, which he will re-record for us. It's wonderful for me, after all these years, to find that someone bothered to keep something of my childhood and, more than that, to discover that these people cared deeply about us, to the point that the woman told me that she had been searching for me for years. After the 'Dear Daughter' programme on television, she left several messages at Goldenbridge Convent, asking the nuns to get a message to me. They never did.

By coincidence, and unknown to me, the girl who was with me there had also decided to visit them, after all these years, just a week before I did. We're all very happy about this but also sad that we lost so much of each other's lives.

A family from Rathgar arrived in Goldenbridge one night when we were all in bed, and although I already had 'a lady', for some reason I was allocated to them. I was sent for, so I got dressed and went to the parlour to be introduced to the parents. Although I liked the family on sight, I recall telling a nun that I didn't want a 'new lady'. The family left, but some days later arrived to take me out for the weekend, which I enjoyed. Two of their children were of a similar age and we got on well. We went off with other children to raid local orchards which I thought was really exciting. I lost touch with this family as a child, but they renewed contact with me soon after the 'Dear Daughter' programme, and we meet occasionally.

Another family, in Crumlin, took me out for weekends and holidays for some years. They had grown-up children, male and female, all of whom I liked, but I became quite close to one of their sons, who was always very kind and gentle with me. We went for long walks along the canal, which I enjoyed. In my teens, whenever I got the chance, I would phone the woman to ask her to phone the orphanage so that I could go out at weekends. Both always obliged, but on one occasion I was horrified to hear one of the nuns warning this kind woman to be careful lest I'd have men queuing up at the door! I was mortified. I never told the woman I had overheard the conversation, but I often wondered what she thought. After I left Goldenbridge, I visited this family occasionally. Just prior to my twenty-first birthday, I visited and, while at the house, suddenly became violently ill. The woman put me to bed, called a doctor and ended up nursing me for an entire week while I recovered from a serious infection. She gave me so much nurturing and good mothering that I spent much of that week in floods of tears, realising how much of this I had missed in my life. Emotionally, I was in extreme turmoil as I struggled to accept her kindness, but felt extremely guilty also about being a burden on her.

St Joseph's Holiday Home

Those of us who didn't have parents or families to take us out for holidays in the summertime, spent them in Rathdrum. This was the holiday home which we always said was ours, because we reckoned it was paid for from money the nuns made on the rosary beads which we made. There were four distinct and separate buildings in Rathdrum. The main building, a large mansion, didn't have a name. An old, though bright and airy structure, the lower floor housed the main hall, oratory, nuns' parlour, dining room, kitchen and scullery. A stairs, immediately to the right of the front hall, led to three medium-sized, comfortable, brightly painted dormitories. There were bathrooms attached to each bedroom.

The second, St Ann's, was a smaller building, which shared its back wall with the local Protestant church and graveyard. It was dark and dull there. Downstairs was the Rec of Rathdrum, as well as the laundry and toilets. The top floor comprised one large dormitory, divided in two by the stairs. For some reason, this dormitory, unlike the others, had campbeds which were extremely uncomfortable.

The cottage, a two-storey cramped building, was used exclusively as a dormitory for the wet-the-beds. The pre-fab, the smallest and the most modern of the buildings, served as additional dormitory space as well as a TV room.

In Rathdrum life was usually easier. Our holidays there gave us significant respite from the relentless cruelty of Goldenbridge. Several factors may have contributed to this. The weather was consistently better, there was a lot more outdoor space, and there were fewer children. On arrival the nuns and staff became instantly more relaxed and humane. We children responded well to these changes in the adults around us and there was far less pressure and stress on us because we were not being bullied and battered so much. I've no doubt the nuns and staff enjoyed their work much more, as a result. This could be seen by the fact that they played outdoor games with us, tended the gardens, took us for walks in the countryside where we enjoyed picking berries, and brought us to the beach at Brittas Bay. We could play much more freely, and routines were somewhat more relaxed. The fact that there was more space meant that we children felt less crowded by each other, and we could go off and have some time alone. We felt less constricted in every way.

There was a steep hill at the back of the main building (now the site of Parnell Park), which we took full advantage of. We'd make a run, grab the branch of a tree and swing all the way down the steep hill. The hard bit came next, walking back up the hill, but we would repeat this over and over again, such was the level of our enjoyment.

The nuns sometimes abandoned whatever they were doing and joined in playing outdoor games with us, but sometimes these potentially fun occasions would turn sour. One day one of them was playing tennis with one of the children. In the process, she struck the ball, sending it in the direction of the child, who missed it. The ball continued on its merry way, towards the Protestant church. To the nun's horror, it struck and damaged a window. Whether it was that she was afraid or annoyed, she turned to the child and said: 'Now look what you've done. Why didn't you hit the ball? There's a bed over in the cottage that needs a mackintosh. Go over there and put it on the bed, for the day.' This was her punishment and the child did as she was told. The trouble was that it only took a few minutes. So, she flattened it, tidied it, removed it, replaced it, but there was only so much of this she could do. Finally, she returned to the play area. The nun's response to seeing her was: 'What are you doing back here? Didn't I tell you to do something for the day?' Typical!

One Sunday, when I was about 12, my father arrived in Rathdrum. He was alone, which was most unusual, as for a few years he used to drive my mother to Rathdrum to see us. He took me to Smyth's, the local sweet shop. At the time, I had a perfectly good black leather strap on my watch, but he decided for some reason to buy me a new brown one. He removed the black strap and put on the new one. As he put the watch back on my wrist, he told me: 'This is the last thing I'll ever buy you. In fact, this is the last time I'll ever see you.' I didn't know what to think or say about this, so I didn't respond to him at all. He walked me back to St Joseph's and drove off. I must have been mulling this over in my head, because about half an hour later, I just burst into tears and pulled the watch from my wrist. I tore the strap off the watch and threw it away. I was very upset. Some of the girls came over and asked me what was wrong. I remember, for some reason, feeling utterly ashamed, and I couldn't tell them. It was almost 20 years before I could bring myself to tell anybody what had happened that day, such was the hurt, shame and humiliation I felt about my father abandoning me, again. What was most peculiar about this scenario was that my mother always told me that I was my father's favourite child. I'm not sure if I ever felt special in his eyes, but I do know that he never beat me. However, even as a young child I knew that he was very unreliable – he would promise to bring us things and he always forgot. The one promise he made, and kept to his death, was this one that he would never see me again or ever buy me anything.

Mass was also part of the daily routine in Rathdrum. We were not in theory expected to attend every day, but if we didn't some adult was very likely to say, 'I didn't see you at mass this morning', so it was easier to go. The atmosphere of the oratory was rather relaxed, and when we got bored, there was the nice scenery surrounding us, and we could see the trees from which we would later swing to the valley below. We were still prone to fainting and a friend of mine recollects that when she was about 9 years old a nun told her that she had deliberately fainted, as an excuse, to go outside to see the milkman!

Laundry and other facilities were not so good, but though I hated chores in Rathdrum for this reason, it was a small price to pay for the relative peace and quiet we enjoyed there. I found the time there a considerable relief for my overloaded and weary nervous system.

At the edge of the grounds there was a gap. This eventually led to a wooded area, which was just like a fairy glade. When we were about 10 years old, some of us went to it, to play, and to sit and talk. We had to get down on all fours to get through the shrubbery which led to it. We were attracted to the beautiful wild flowers. We admired the colours and fine texture of the petals and we ate sour leaves. The secret to the continued enjoyment of this experience was to remember to go back on time for meals, which we always managed to achieve. I don't know whether or not the nuns and staff were aware of our secret hideout, but if they were, they never stopped us going.

Because I liked this place so much, one day I went down on my own. As usual, beautiful flowers greeted me, while butterflies flew all around them. I came upon a small grassed area, shaped like a hammock, with perfectly placed arm rests. Lying down and soaking up the heat of the sun, I felt as safe and secure as if I were being held by an angel's wings. There I lay for a long while, feeling completely relaxed in mind and body. With eyes closed, mind at rest, and listening to the sounds of the forest, I relished the undisturbed and peaceful atmosphere of this space. That, for me, was the happiest experience of my time in the care of the Sisters of Mercy. It is the only conscious memory I retain of feeling utterly at peace and free from the considerable strains and worries of my life.

Pressure and tension ran high as always at mealtimes and bedtimes. These routines were as regimental and harsh as in

Goldenbridge. But the quality of the food was better. Too much harm couldn't be done to summer foods like salads, though the portions were often too small. It is true to say that, at the very least, Rathdrum was definitely a holiday home in comparison to the continuous reign of terror at Goldenbridge. There was one significant exception – when it rained! On the lower floor of St Ann's building there was a room with a bench on all four walls, just like the Rec. Here we were subjected to similar, though not quite so vicious, beatings by some of the staff. I think the fact that the nuns were present on site, most of the time, may have acted as a restraint on the staff.

Some of the older girls were more interested in sneaking out, past an old unused cottage, just inside the main gates. This led directly on to the main street, where the girls would meet local lads and get to know the town. One such group of boys, whom the nuns definitely disapproved of, were the 'Foxies'. They regularly climbed the walls to sit and talk with us. Occasionally they'd bring ice creams to share with us. They were often caught and there was a constant game of cat and mouse, between the 'Foxies', us, and the nuns, but these lads were harmless.

One nun seemed to like the outdoor life. She tended the garden and rockery, actively encouraging us to help, though it was a task I did not enjoy. I was afraid of creeping creatures in the ground, and I preferred to play. She regularly took us on walks to Avondale where, with buckets in hand, we spent long hours picking berries. I enjoyed this much more, partly because we could eat the berries.

Going to the beach was a great adventure. Brittas Bay was full of dunes and sharp grass, and we loved it. The nuns always took us to the beach and once we were settled they, for reasons of modesty, headed off into the far distance to change into their swimwear. We, curious children that we were, would follow them with our eyes. All we could see though, were two white heads bopping up and down in the water. They always returned fully attired in their religious habits.

Jam sandwiches were the staple diet on beach days. On windy days we were invariably treated to the sand-tasting variety, but we relished them anyway. Sweets, of course, always held our interest. There are countless stories about stealing sweets when the nuns were resting in the parlour in the early evening. Most of us got away with this, but occasionally some were unlucky enough to get caught, even after getting away with the sweets. One night, two girls were so busy sharing their booty, that they didn't notice anyone listening to them as one said to the other, 'One for you and two for me, because I robbed them.' A particular nun then proceeded to slap them, saying, 'One for you and two for you because you robbed them.' That's the risk we took!

After healthy, active days in Rathdrum, we were usually quite tired and so the staff had less trouble getting us to sleep. The exception to this was the dormitory in St Ann's. It was very uncomfortable to sleep there, firstly because of the camp-beds. They were made of a sheet of canvas and two bars. There was no support as the canvas was only about an inch thick, and we'd regularly fall through the base as the bars collapsed. Secondly, we kept imagining we could hear banshees in the Protestant graveyard, just outside the windows. The smaller children would be upset and start to cry while the big girls played on their fears, exaggerating and adding to stories passed down through the years.

All good things come to an end and we faced the inevitable, bravely. Our return to Goldenbridge was by coach and we sang heartily all the way back. Often, on arrival at the main gates, the singing was temporarily brought to an abrupt end while stones were being thrown at the coaches by young residents of the notorious Keogh's Square which faced the entrance to Goldenbridge. With windows shattering and splinters of glass sticking in us, we ducked and dived to avoid being injured. The young children screamed with fright and these incidents marked perfectly our re-introduction to the fear and terror we associated with Goldenbridge. Still, we recovered sufficiently to sing yet again the final song, as the coach approached the orphanage.

> Cheer up Goldenbridge, it's known everywhere,
> We left poor Rathdrum and left it lying there,
> And we all called for mercy, and mercy wasn't there,
> Cheer up Goldenbridge, it's known everywhere.

It's striking how prophetic those lyrics were. I think it is ironic that, as a result of the stories which in recent years emerged from Goldenbridge, the place has indeed come to be widely known.

CHAPTER EIGHT

– Growing Pains –

As we got older we became more aware of all the mannerisms and habits, especially verbal, of all those working in the orphanage. One of the nuns was small, pleasantly plump, and had many unusual personal habits. These included rubbing her hands, which were chubby, as if she was cold. I used to think, later, that it was a way of comforting herself. She was always pulling at her cardigan, bringing the two sides of it together, firmly in front of her, but never fastening the buttons. Fiddling with her wimple, she used to keep pushing an imaginary piece of hair up under it, on top of her forehead. She always wore what we termed 'granny's shoes', big round-toed ones in the winter and sandals with vertical and horizontal straps, with toes peeking out, in the summer.

She had a pleasant smile and was capable of laughter. She smiled at some children, and she particularly liked babies, even treating some of them as 'pets'. She was kinder than others, and she didn't hit or beat us with the same savagery.

During this period we would be called a litany of names, none of which was flattering. These included: ninny hammer, *amadán*, *óinseach*, twit, gombeen, crackawley, half-wit, puss-face, rogue. We didn't know what some of the names meant, but we did know they were designed to insult us and make us feel bad. They used to tell me that I was a half-wit. This really hurt, and I thought about it for a long time afterwards, wondering what exactly a half-wit was. Other expressions used regularly to me were: 'You're capable of anything, Fahy', and 'I wouldn't expect any better of you.' They sound like contradictions, but the former was meant in a negative sense.

Whenever one of the adults was threatening us, she used to tell us: 'I'll beat you till you're black and blue' and 'Woe betide you' and 'Just draw me on you'. When it came to actually hitting us, she used to send us out to get the hand-brush with which she was going to beat us. Her words ring in my ears to this day. 'Get me a hand-brush and don't come back and tell me you couldn't find one.' When we tried that, she'd send someone else off, usually our friends, threatening them that if they couldn't find one, she would, and they would get a beating too. Naturally, we'd display signs of upset and she'd shout, 'Take that sulk off your face.' When she did hit us with the hand-brush and other implements, she knew how to hurt. We would immediately put our hands under the pit of our arms, to comfort ourselves from the stinging and throbbing.

Public Humiliation

There are, as too many children know, many ways to be cruel and the really damaging ways do not have to include physical attack. Public humiliation was the favourite device of many the staff and of the nuns. The humiliation was particularly vicious for girls who were maturing into women. One person never missed such an opportunity. It was as if she just couldn't help herself. Her comments always centred around our existence, our bodily functions, and our sexuality. A friend of mine from those days, who always made such an effort to be 'very good', recalls how insulted she felt, and how she'd want to sink into the ground, when she was regularly told: 'There's a smell of BO off you.'

Even younger children weren't spared. There was the on-going issue of wetting the bed and of young boys, in particular, soiling themselves. One nun, on realising something of this nature had happened, would shout, with nose uplifted and fingers holding it, 'Who did that destroy?' A strange phrase indeed! The younger children would be terrified. In fairness to her, she didn't always beat them for it, but she would call them dirty and tell them they were disgusting and the like. More commonly, what caused these unpleasant smells was the lack of toilet paper. Early in the day, one might find cut squares of newspaper hanging on a nail in the toilets. Very soon, however, there would be none and children resorted to all sorts of creative ways of dealing with what was an obvious problem. Eventually, the institution began to supply loo paper of the glass-feeling variety (similar to that found at the time in the toilets of trains), which we christened CIÉ paper. As on train toilets, there was never enough of it.

I remember very well a girl who must have developed a hormonal imbalance because she was maturing rapidly, and one effect of this was that she sweated profusely. She washed herself the same as the rest of us, but she did have this problem. Almost every day she was humiliated in front of us, her peers and told how dirty and disgusting she was. At times she was forced to strip down to her underwear in front of us, then despatched to the washroom. The poor girl cringed through this ordeal. So did we. Her humiliation was thorough, and as I watched this abusive behaviour, I hated the authorities and all that they stood for. They seemed terrified of our budding femininity and were at a loss to know how to cope with it. On the other hand, some of them seemed also to be very curious about it and I thought, even then, that this behaviour was inconsistent, to say the least.

I recall, for example, that in one of the new buildings there were showers and that one person in authority would regularly, without warning, pull back curtains, as she said herself, 'To see who is in there.' She seemed particularly curious about breasts and if she met a teenager with ample breasts running along the corridor, she would invariably tell her she was a disgrace and to go and put a bra on. In those days, the idea of padded bras to enhance one's figure was catching on, and was disapproved of by the nuns. This individual was known to call girls to a room and literally feel their breasts, as she said, to find out if they were padded. The girls naturally hated this and to this day feel extremely angry about it.

This was all happening at a time when, if we noticed a slight pimple on our faces, we couldn't wait to buy the next jar of Valderma cream for spots. We felt so grown-up and normal when we asked a girl who went to the shops for the nuns, to buy it. Our first bras, suspender belts and nylon stockings were all bought by this girl from Lavin's drapery shop in Inchicore. Our first choice of colour in nylons was 'gypsy-gold' and gave the instant impression of sheer tanned legs which had the amazing effect of enhancing our self image. Of course, only those of us with money provided by parents and host families could indulge in these luxuries but we were generally willing to share our goodies, at least with our friends.

So while we did those normal things, we had to endure the abnormal ordeal of the ritualistic painting of our bodies, for the treatment of scabies. This was done to us on a weekly basis for years, by nuns and staff members. It was utterly degrading. One of them, somehow, always chose to paint the bodies of pre-pubescent teenagers. She would humiliate them by telling them that they were disgusting and should be painting their own bodies, because they were maturing. By the same token, if they had taken the liberty of painting their own bodies, she would also berate and humiliate them for thinking they were mature enough to do so, so she always won that battle. Given that we had been brainwashed about 'modesty' and, in the process, become ashamed of our bodies, she added to our pain. She did this, as we experienced it, by gawking at us, ordering us to turn round while ignoring our obvious discomfort.

Everything about the body was cloak-and-dagger stuff. I'll never forget the underwear changing sessions. Urine and faeces stains were displayed on a pole for our peers to see and affirm that they were dirty. Beatings and humiliations always followed, but the shame was the worst part of all. To avoid these experiences, most of us washed our underwear when everyone was gone to bed. We sneaked to the toilets which had long ago lost the lid of their cisterns, and washed them. Having done this, we put them between the mattress and the sheet we lay on, to dry. Most often, they were still wet in the morning and we put them on us like this. That's how desperate we had become to avoid the ritualistic, masochistic behaviour of the adults who were supposed to be caring for us. The cisterns we used for washing our underwear were the same ones we used to drink water from, day and night, when we were thirsty. Water was never provided at mealtimes and we didn't dare ask for it. So, using our hands, we scooped up the freezing water and drank it. It's a wonder we didn't get all the diseases under the sun.

We were always discouraged from allowing others to catch sight of our flesh, particularly our genitalia. We were told to hunch down under school desks to change our underwear, and it's amazing how adept we became at avoiding seeing each other's bodies. One of the problems with this was the inconsistency of the adults' behaviour, which was confusing. On paint and bath days, we were lined up, naked, regardless of age, one behind the other, while awaiting our turn. We were then shoved into a scalding hot bath or a freezing cold one, depending on where we were in the queue. As a result of having my head regularly shoved down into baths, I suffered the very distressing feeling of drowning, while showering, for many years after I left Goldenbridge.

Periodic Episodes

Practically every female who went through the Goldenbridge regime remembers the day their first period arrived. For most of us, it was a surprise and a serious worry, even though some of us had heard tell of it on the grapevine. Girls who left before me have told me that it was horrendous for them. They had only got so many towels each and had to maintain them. I can only begin to imagine what that was like, with the lack of washing facilities in those days.

I was in the Sacred Heart dormitory toilets when mine came. Even though I guessed what the problem was, I didn't know for sure and I certainly didn't know the rituals and procedures involved. But I soon learned. Feeling somewhat panicked, I rushed out and told a friend, who confirmed my worst fears – my 'grannys' had arrived. I was very confused. On the one hand, I felt somewhat grown up and normal, and on the other, I felt ashamed and dirty, about bleeding from God knows where. I also had a terrible pain in my stomach, and my friend told me this was normal, and that I'd probably get the pain every month.

We had to go to the staff member in charge of the medicine press and ask for a sanitary towel. This meant having to give her private information about ourselves and we all hated that. Standing in line outside St Philomena's, and copying from the more learned bigger girls, I took my towel. Like them, I shoved it quickly and secretly up my sleeve, and left the intimidating scene. The next big question was, What do I do with this? There's many a story about girls taking one another into the cloakroom and showing them what to do. We'd lend each other ST belts so that we wouldn't have to ask the staff member who, for whatever reason, didn't offer one on the first occasion. The girls were nice to each other about periods. We didn't frighten or scare younger ones any more than was 'normal' in the atmosphere we lived in. What we learned about periods, which included describing them as 'grannys', 'Auntie Marys', and 'me friends,' was very much a case of hit-and-miss. We were told nothing about the menstrual cycle, or the connection between it and other aspects of sexuality, such as the all-important one of when and how one becomes pregnant.

Some girls found out more when the mother in their host family told them, but that was rare. Most of us didn't understand any of that, but we were probably no different to many other teenagers in the Ireland of the 1960s. We were preoccupied trying to cope with the practical aspects of it and rather than keep asking for an ST every time we needed one, we took to using rags and paper, which wasn't very pleasant.

In later years, things progressed somewhat and the nuns and staff gave us a full pack of sanitary towels. This reduced the shame and feeling of intimidation somewhat, and it was a great relief. It meant though that there was a bigger risk that the younger girls would find them, as indeed they did. I recall a scene in Rathdrum, during a summer's evening. A young girl appeared with a sanitary towel hooked onto her ears, and worn like a hair-band. Then she switched it to her mouth which made it look like a doctor's mask. A nun caught her and threatened to 'crown her', but the rest of us thought it was hilariously funny.

The Facts of Life

When one of the nuns decided to tell us the facts of life, everybody over the age of 13 was told to be in her classroom at a particular time. It was summer. We sat at our desks. One girl, who was older than me, arrived slightly late, looking terribly nervous, because she really was in fear of this nun. 'And where do you think you're going?' the nun demanded. 'I'm coming to the talk, Sister,' the girl said nervously. 'Indeed, you're not,' the nun retorted. 'You don't need it.' And the poor girl went off, told yet again, in effect, that she had no place among decent people. I never heard from this girl since and I often wonder how she came to terms with these experiences, if indeed she ever did.

The facts of life, as we heard them, were nothing short of nonsense. The nun sat at the top of the room looking very awkward and uncomfortable. She never mentioned the word sex but did mention the term intercourse, without explaining the mechanics of sex, or how one became pregnant. She showed a couple of slides, which included one of a man and woman kissing. This she told us, allowing a man to put his tongue in your mouth, is what leads to pregnancy. It was followed by a second slide, a woman holding the baby. There was no man in that slide.

Perhaps the nuns believed that the less we knew about sex, the less likely we were to become curious about it and, worse still, actively engage it in. After all, their principal aim was to protect us from moral danger, and they achieved this by feeding us a diet of asexual manna, investing huge amounts of energy in teaching us the value of remaining chaste so that we would emulate the lives of nuns and live as 'virgins most pure'. In contrast to their theoretical teaching, in practice they continually punished us for being the product of our parents' sin and predicted that we would 'turn out' just like our mothers. One friend of mine who had attended that talk, told me that subsequently this piece of information was to haunt her. Having engaged in french kissing with her boyfriend, she lay awake night after night, terrified, while awaiting her next period, in case she had become pregnant.

The nun did, however, talk a good deal about rape. This I found terrifying. She outlined the temptations women brought to men, the way they walked on beaches dressed only in bikinis, for example. She said such women were looking for rape and deserved rape. She warned us that men couldn't control themselves, and therefore 'couldn't help it'. She talked of them getting carried away. After the initial 'talk', she provided a box into which we could put questions. To illustrate how much we had learned about the 'facts of life', one girl asked, 'Could you get pregnant if you sat on a bus seat after a man?'

This talk went a long way towards re-enforcing ideas I already had that being female was dangerous, that I was a temptation to men, and that therefore I must be bad. I now came to the belief that men couldn't control themselves, that they must be like animals. This was typical of the so-called sex education of girls in Ireland of those years, often imparted both at home and in schools. I recall feeling really frightened and angry with men as a result, and I found them extremely threatening. I decided that it was best to just avoid them. I couldn't believe, and wouldn't accept, that they were so powerless over their sexual behaviour, and I hated them for the threat they posed to me. I was perfectly aware that men were physically stronger than me and this added to my feelings of helplessness. I felt it wasn't safe to be a woman and, as a result, I resented very deeply having been born female.

This coincided with and re-affirmed in my mind the talks we were receiving in the secondary school, about men who couldn't control their sexual urges. For many a long year after this, I worked hard at avoiding men. I had become afraid of them. The distorted information I received impacted very seriously on my sexual development and contributed significantly to my fast-growing dread of men. I presume it affected others in similar ways. For that, and for my subsequent inability to develop and maintain good relationships with men, I feel extremely angry.

Sexual Awareness

In the mid-sixties the Irish economy was beginning to expand and some of it rubbed off on Goldenbridge. Buildings were refurbished and pre-fabs were added. This meant there were men, other than priests, around the place, and we as teenagers were naturally curious about them. We were innocent about them though and one Saturday morning, before breakfast, one of the nuns caught some of us waving to the workmen, through closed windows, along the corridor. She sent for us, and when we arrived in her office, the workmen were already there. She simply announced to them that we, who were present, were man-mad. I thought that was an outrageous thing to do. It seemed to say more about her mind than it did about ours. It was utterly humiliating for us and we were mortified. We thought that the men believed her and, besides, it was an extremely dangerous and foolish thing for her to do.

There was a young workman who had a long fringe, which he flicked back in what seemed a really hip, macho and even sexy way. We used to try to flip our hair in the same way. One day he was working at the base of the furnace. Two of the girls, on the roof of the furnace, spotted him. They 'chatted him up', and he began asking them questions. As one of them related to me later: 'We were trying to be mod, leaning on the stairway, trying to act "the ladies". We wanted him to fancy us. We gave him the impression we were living in a hotel. We told him we didn't have to do any work, that cleaners came in to do all that. We didn't want him thinking we were only skivvies.' Unfortunately, a nun overheard the entire conversation, and in front of the workman she turned to them and said: 'Well, the toilets down the end of the yard, and the toilets in the Rec need to be cleaned. Go down now and clean them.' And so their sojourn into fantasy land ended.

Another regular fantasy of ours was that there were men climbing over the low walls outside our dormitory. Whispers would fly through the place and one night I went so far as to get the sweeping brush which was always stored in the wardrobe. Hiding behind the curtained entrance to the dormitory and hearing footsteps coming nearer, I lashed out with the brush. Luckily I missed and found, to my horror, a nun standing in front of me. I don't know which of us got the biggest fright, but she ordered me back to bed and we girls laughed about that for a long time afterwards.

Some incidents which happened in the same dormitory were not funny at all. One of the staff, who for years had actively participated in the 'Rec scenes', was on duty. By now we had long feared and hated her. One night she caught one of us playing a game we called 'bicycles', while lying on her bed. She beat her up so badly that the girl's screams could be heard throughout the entire six dormitories of the building. Even we, who were used to so much violence, thought this was beyond all limits. A few nights later, she caught me, in my nightdress, sitting with my back to the wall, on a corner bed, talking with the others in the dormitory. She pulled me by the hair to my feet, stripped me naked in front of my peers, and beat me viciously. Then she just walked away. I felt dreadful after that. I climbed into bed, more battered and bruised that I'd ever felt in my life. I thought I was capable of taking anything that was thrown at me, until that night. As I lay on my bed, trying to sleep, I knew I had reached my limit. I genuinely thought that I was going to crack up, disintegrate, and never come back. I had reached the end of the line. I couldn't take anymore.

I fell asleep after a while, but some hours later, I was awoken by the sound of screams, my own screams. With bedclothes on the floor, a migraine headache that was blowing my head off, and an earache, I recalled earlier events, and just wanted to die. It was an extremely rare event to disturb the nuns from their sleep, but somebody went to get one of them because I was in such a state. She arrived in the dormitory and the girls told her what had happened that night, and a few nights earlier with the other girl. The nun didn't ever discuss it with me, but whatever transpired, this staff member and others left the orphanage. We came to the conclusion that she and others of her ilk were let go.

Something about this incident almost destroyed me at that time. I think it was a combination of factors: the shame it induced in me at the age of 13, the damage it did to my self-esteem, the fact that I was rendered absolutely powerless in the face of such a vicious assault. Fundamentally, it was about the breaking of my spirit. In the immediate aftermath of this event, a very significant one in my life, I actively withdrew from everybody and became extremely depressed. I could no longer see any point in my life and I swore I would kill myself. Every Sunday when I went out with my mother, I met with my twin, Michael, on whom I relied for support and love. I'd tell him that as soon as he left me I was going to throw myself in the river Liffey. I absolutely meant it and I only wished I had the courage to do it. Then I'd berate myself for that. I'd tell myself I was gutless after all, that I couldn't even do that! The only thing that kept me alive in spirit was the love I had for my brothers. I hated every adult who walked the earth. I had given up on them all. It seemed that not one of them cared about me enough and, finally, I had allowed the truth to dawn on me. I never told Michael what had happened to me that awful night. In fact I didn't tell anybody for many years. I felt too embarrassed and ashamed because I hadn't been able to defend myself. This incident, I have no doubt, significantly marred my life, for many, many years afterwards.

I never told my mother any of this. Afternoons with her had become mere rituals, full of superficial exchanges. These often included criticism from her of my clothes, of how I walked with a stoop and so on, thus adding to the misery I felt inside the walls of Goldenbridge.

When I left Goldenbridge I continually searched for this woman. I looked at everybody who got on a bus. I searched people's faces in the city when I went to town. I determined in my mind that if I ever saw her I would kill her, such was my hatred of her. I'm glad now that our paths have never crossed since. If I ever see her, I will ensure that she takes the time to sit down with me while we go over the events of that night, and as she listens to what I have to say, that she goes through that agony with me, so that she will know what it felt like to have one's spirit completely shattered.

Boys

Outside Goldenbridge some of us met boys whom we liked. My brothers were living in St Saviour's Boys' Home, in Dominick Street and when I was about 12 my twin brother was ill in bed. St Saviour's being a much freer environment, I was allowed visit him in his room. There I met some other boys who were also unwell. Amongst them was a boy I grew very close to. I'm not sure whether or not I seriously considered him to be my boyfriend, but I certainly liked him a lot and we regularly went for long walks together around the city centre. He also had sisters in Goldenbridge as well as another brother in St Saviour's, so we had a lot in common. We didn't talk much about the respective orphanages we lived in, and I was conscious not to say much about Goldenbridge because I didn't want him to be upset about his sisters. We often talked of what we would like to do with our futures and we planned to be together as soon as both of us were 'free'. That wasn't to be.

One day, while in the beads class, the newspaper was as usual brought in for the staff, and the headline said that three boys had died in a swimming tragedy in Donegal. It named them and that's how I knew that my friend was one of them. I remember feeling the shock, and I left the room. I didn't talk to anybody in Goldenbridge about it, not even his sisters, but I did talk to Michael about it, incessantly, when we met on Sundays. We spent hours walking around the city centre, every Sunday, and I always threatened to throw myself in the Liffey. How my poor brother dealt with this threat at the time, I don't know.

He has told me since that he was very worried about it. Naturally, I feel that I shouldn't have worried him in this way, but like so many threats of this nature, I meant it at the time. I know, in retrospect, that it was a cry for help. I was desperately unhappy and I missed this boy terribly.

In the meantime, his sisters had been told by an uncle that their two brothers and a friend had drowned just hours after arriving in Donegal. One of the nuns was present and when their uncle left she gave them two bull's eyes sweets and told them to go and say their prayers. Later in the day, the elder sister, upset and crying, was scrubbing a floor on hands and knees. All she could think was, This couldn't be true. Her brothers had visited them the previous day and had brought them a sponge cake. While struggling with her shock and grief, one of the staff came along and, seeing her crying, slapped her hard across the face and told her to stop that silly nonsense. To this day, on the anniversary of her brothers' deaths, she insists on being absolutely alone. She feels that she still hasn't grieved properly and can't file it away. It didn't help that the day her brothers died was a year to the day after she and her family had been taken into care when their mother abandoned them.

Another friend recalls that a nun, while slapping her across the face for talking to a painter, accused her of having sex with him. This would seem to indicate that she saw the possibility that sex could occur between us and the men, but if she did she didn't act on it. Knowing the nuns as we did, the chances were that if she found out, she would have blamed us anyway. What is known is that at least two of the workmen employed by the nuns in this era and one female member of staff were sexually abusing a number of girls. So while some endured this and others of us were seriously at risk, some of the nuns could speculate about us engaging in sex, but never dream of trying to ensure that we were safe. This nun truly believed that all of us girls were man-mad. She always thought in those terms. For example, one girl developed a sty in her eye when she was about 14. The nun told her she got this from looking at German sailors, who had taken us out for the day, while their ship visited Dublin port!

When I was 15, while on holiday in Northern Ireland with relatives, I thought about the nuns and their warnings. I met a boy who was part of a group that I became friendly with. It was during the early days of the Troubles, and I was staying with Catholic relatives in a predominantly Protestant area. The group I met with were mixed but there was some banter about religious allegiances and this made me very nervous, as I wasn't used to it. I'd always learned that Protestants would go straight to hell, and I was somewhat afraid of them for this reason.

This boy linked up with me because, as he said, we had the same religion. We became very friendly and somewhat more intimate over the following weeks. During these times, I remember feeling extremely guilty and wondered what the nuns would say if they knew. One thing was sure though, they weren't going to hear it from me. Partly because I lived in an orphanage, he and I didn't maintain contact, but I was back in Dublin a few months when once again I found out through the newspapers that he too had died. Naturally this upset me very much. I didn't talk to anybody in depth about it, though I remember having a brief conversation with my mother who did seem to understand my loss. This, together with my previous loss, left a deep impression on me, in that I seriously began to think I was jinxed in some way. These losses, together with all the stuff the nuns had brainwashed us with, led me to believe that it would be better to stay away from boys, because it was just too painful and too complicated.

Shameful Background

The attacks on our parents – mostly our mothers, because our fathers were very rarely mentioned – played a crucial part in our growing up. When nuns and staff told us, 'You'll turn out like your mother,' they meant it as an attack on us, pointing out an inherent, irredeemable flaw: our birth. We all knew our mothers were not the Virgin Mary, or nuns. We were told that our parents did something bad and we were the products of this. On that basis alone, we were shameful people. We were told plainly that we would be no good, that our mothers were prostitutes, and that we'd be fit for nothing else but going on the streets.

We were also informed that if our mothers could manage things better, then we wouldn't be here. That too was shameful. Some of our mothers were too poor to manage alone in a world where men, usually their husbands, could abandon them and their children, without consequence. Some were physically or mentally ill. Some were exhausted from alcoholic husbands. And some just didn't care. Others cared very much indeed and some fathers too tried very hard to keep their families together. Even when they were succeeding, many were pressurised by priests and nuns to have their children looked after better by the good nuns. We, the children, suffered the consequences, and carried the shame for our parents, for the Church and indeed for all of Irish society.

The nuns made it clear to us that we were a burden on them. I felt shamed and guilty when we were regularly told the price of the bread bill. We were told again and again how difficult it was to meet the cost of keeping us. With a child's logic, I used to wonder why they wouldn't just kill us and end it for us. After all, they didn't seem to relish looking after us and, as we used to say so often, we didn't ask to be born or to be in Goldenbridge.

Shame was definitely a major part of the control system. A

sense of shame would ensure that we didn't develop notions about ourselves or our 'true', lowly station in life. This shame was especially induced in females. And it worked. Most of us left with the signs of it displayed across our whole being – stooped shoulders, heads directed at the ground, lack of self-esteem and not a shred of confidence. I was ashamed of being 'illegitimate', and I thought and felt I hadn't the right to exist. There are some pains which all of us at some time or other find indescribable, and I'll never forget the anguish I felt deep inside me about this aspect of my life. I don't believe I could ever begin accurately to convey to another human being the deep shame and pain I felt about this as a child and for many, many years after I left Goldenbridge.

During the 'facts of life' talk and at every other opportunity, the nuns scared us off men. But one of them would then turn on us, saying, 'You'll jump on the first man when you're out of here and you'll be back here in trouble.' A girl who had left a year before us came back to visit. One nun brought her to our classroom, and related a story. She told us: 'There was a girl who left here not all that long ago and she got herself into trouble. I'm not naming any names.' All of us, including this girl's sister, assumed that the story was about her. The poor girl was standing there in front of us all, not looking pregnant, but certainly down-at-heel and shame-faced. I've no doubt that she had enough to deal with without being subjected to this humiliation! One might wonder why girls came back to visit the nuns. The simple answer is that they had nowhere else to go. They needed financial and emotional support. I've no idea what support they did get, but what I do know is that no one ever said to us, 'Come back and see us if you find yourself in any difficulties.' We were just dumped out on the world without a clue how to manage in it.

I've often thought about the Virgin Mary in this context, and I've wondered what would have become of her if she'd been raised in Goldenbridge and found herself to be 'with child'. How would she have begun to explain to the nuns that she was 'in trouble', and that her child was of God, as a result of an immaculate conception? Given that she was 'betrothed' to Joseph, I've no doubt that in the Ireland of the 1960s, he'd have been given his walking papers, she would have ended up in a Magdalen home, and, God help us, Jesus might have ended up in Goldenbridge. I wonder how they'd have treated him!

When they left Goldenbridge, most of the girls took the first boat to England, usually ending up in London. On their return, pregnant or otherwise, the nuns would ask them if they had any advice to give us. Most commonly they'd say that London was a lonely place for girls on their own. This was just what the nuns wanted to hear and it affirmed their oft quoted dictum, that 'only bad girls went to London'.

Many a girl who was raised in Goldenbridge has told me of her ignorance about all matters sexual and feminine. One girl, one of the 'big girls' when I was small, was, in 1968, married, pregnant, and aged 24. She told me that she hadn't a clue what part of her body the child was going to come out of. On discovering, during the process of giving birth, where babies emerged from, she found it to be the most embarrassing experience of her life. 'I didn't expect it to come from my private parts,' she said.

Combined with the lack of information was an obsession with maintaining our purity. One girl, aged 14, was suffering acute migraine headaches when she awoke each morning. She was so ill that she was vomiting and eventually one of the staff reported it to a nun. A doctor, whom we had never seen before, arrived and examined her stomach and breasts. In hindsight, she realised she had been examined to confirm whether or not she was pregnant! Nothing more was ever said or done about her migraines, which continued for some time afterwards.

Real Families

Meanwhile, those of us who remained, discovered, as we grew bigger and older, that there was the on-going issue of families and their role in our lives. Some parents were actively discouraged from visiting, and I recall some of the nuns being insulting to some parents. I always felt that they did this to unassertive and poorer families in particular. When we were younger our mothers were told, 'not to come, for the best'. Parents, as a result, might be absent for several years. When they would finally make contact again, one nun would say to the young person, 'They only want you now because you're old enough to go out and work.' While there may well have been some truth in that, and maybe even a lot of truth, it was very confusing for us because we wanted to believe our parents cared. I'm not suggesting that the nuns should have allowed us to live with illusions, or ignorance, but this wasn't the way to deal with it.

'Pop Call'

Sometimes the nuns could be innocent too. I recall one night sitting in St Patrick's watching Pan's People, a dancing group on 'Top of the Pops', when I suddenly heard one of the nuns posing the question, very seriously, 'Is that Bernadette Fahy I see on the television?' Everyone roared laughing at the very idea of it, but she didn't bat an eyelid.

When she was in charge of our small teenage group, we got to listen to records on the record-player. Each group possessed a record-player. Our favourite records included 'Ob-la-di-ob-la-da', 'Sugar, sugar', 'Spirit in the Sky' and Peter Sarstedz's 'Where do you go to my lovely?' Predicting problems, I bought two copies of the latter. One nun was horrified with the lyrics, and she took it and broke it in half. I didn't risk playing the second copy, and still have it.

Some of us had our own transistors by then, and mine was

a great comfort to me. We'd tune into Radio Luxembourg and Radio Caroline. On Wednesday nights we'd listen to RTÉ for 'Pop Call', which we enjoyed very much. Quite often, though, a staff member would tell us to turn off the radio and I'd turn mine down as far as possible and continue to listen to it. Most often I'd fall asleep and the batteries would be wasted, but for me it was worth all the money in the world, such was the pleasure it brought me.

We especially liked listening to the requests on 'Pop Call', which were done in alphabetical order. We longed to have a request played for us. One night, someone dared me to try, and I and some others went downstairs. I rang 'Pop Call' and got through straight away. It wasn't the turn of the letter F that night, but shaking like a leaf, I gave a false name, and put in a request for a gang of us, using only first names. I hoped to God that no one, other than us who were privy to what I had done, would hear it. We were excited and nervous, wondering what would happen if someone, inside or outside of the place, heard it and reported us. The request was played and our fear and anxiety was mixed with the pleasure of hearing our names over the air. It felt like we had connected with the outside world, and it was all the sweeter, with time, because we had beaten the system and got away with it.

Things were improving somewhat in Goldenbridge when we were teenagers. But still I couldn't wait to get out of the place. At 13, I made a deal with a friend in the middle dormitory of Our Lady's. It was that she would help me remember, every day, how many days I had to spend before I left. Each night, we reduced the number by one until, finally, there were no days left. In the midst of this, I experienced a major setback. One Sunday, I arrived down in the porch hall, to find a major structure erected there. It contained an architect's drawing plans for a proposed hostel, complete with a slot for donations. I recall a nun asking my mother if she thought it was a good idea, and whether or not she thought that I might live in it. I was horrified to hear this. My mother went through the motions of agreeing with her, but when we got outside I told her I wouldn't like to live in it, and she agreed that I wouldn't have to.

CHAPTER NINE

– Last Years –

As mentioned earlier, I was one of the lucky people who had the opportunity to attend the outside secondary school also run by the Mercy nuns at Inchicore. I was chosen in the following way. One day a nun came to the classroom in the orphanage and put a long sum on the board. She told us to put up our hands as soon as we had it done. After three of us had done so, she asked for our answer. We all had the same one and she then said, 'You, you, and you, are going to the secondary school after Christmas.'

When we arrived we were assigned to different classes. The other two were taught principally by lay teachers, while my main teacher was a nun.

Those first few weeks were terrifying. We just hadn't a clue. We had already missed the first term, so we had a lot of catching up to do. It soon emerged that we were not quite up to the standard of other students. For example, I was considered good at maths and Irish in the orphanage school but in secondary school I was considered to be a very 'weak' student. It's a term I came to detest. I had always prided myself on being bright at school, and it was confusing and a serious blow to my confidence to be considered otherwise.

It was strange going out to school from the orphanage. The staff and some of the girls didn't appreciate the particular stresses associated with being in secondary school. For instance, we always had lots of homework and it was hard to find enough time to do it.

At school, I didn't feel quite equal to my peers. I was always acutely conscious of the fact that I came from the orphanage, didn't live at home and didn't seem to have parents. I was ambivalent about my peers in class asking me personal questions about why I was in the orphanage and what it was like. It evoked fear. On the other hand, I thought that they had no interest in me when they didn't ask. For these reasons, I became quite introverted and didn't volunteer any information about myself or the orphanage. When the nuns and teachers made reference to the students' parents, for example, threatening to complain about their behaviour, I always felt I had to ensure that such threats wouldn't be made against me. I wanted to avoid any reference to the fact that I came from the orphanage.

Because the head of the school did not approve of uniforms, we wore our own clothes to school. This created some problems, in that it was the mini-skirt era and the nuns hated them. One of them regularly called us 'slaves to fashion', and went as far as taping newspaper onto the base of some of our skirts in order to lengthen them. She was constantly reminding us that we were a source of temptation to men. I felt angry that men would blame us for their sexual temptations and I realise now that all of this indoctrination had a very profound effect on me.

The principal visited each classroom at least once a week. She was an extremely tall and powerful-looking woman, whose back was slightly stooped, giving the impression that she carried the world on her shoulders. She would talk of her busyness and took every opportunity to tell us off for wearing mini-skirts. The wearing of nail varnish, whether plain or coloured, as well as all jewellery, was banned. One of the most serious offences was not to have the fringe of one's hair cut regularly. This posed a problem for me, since in the orphanage we all had fringes, and they were cut when it was decided by the nuns in the orphanage. I was regularly told that it was no wonder I couldn't see with my long fringe. Every day the nun brought clips to the classroom, which she put in my hair. For some reason, she always forgot them on Saturday mornings and I'd regularly be sent back to the orphanage to get some. Since we always did Irish and singing on Saturday mornings, I didn't rush back and I often didn't bother to return at all. But the nun became wise to this and began to remember, even on Saturdays.

In general, those of us who went to the secondary school found it quite demanding. Living in the orphanage, doing all our usual chores, in the mornings, before and after meals, together with the additional strain of lessons, teachers, study and examinations, left us very tense. The one and only work we were spared was the making of rosary beads, sometimes. We still had to make them on Saturdays and on days when, for whatever reason, we were off school but the 'inside' school was still open.

As well as those strains, some of us attending secondary school were by now long considered to be 'big enough' to be put in charge of dormitories. This involved getting up twice a night to get the younger children to the toilets, so our sleep was continually interrupted. It was always difficult to get back to sleep because someone would be talking, snoring or coughing. And so, like I'd learned so well, I'd be saying to the boys in my dormitory, 'Shut up talking whoever that is. Who is that snoring?' When that didn't work, I'd get out of my bed several times a night to pinch the noses of children who, fast asleep, continued to snore. Needless to say, I feel thoroughly ashamed about this now, but it does show how insidious cruelty is, how we learn it, consciously and unconsciously. It really upset me, years later, when I realised just how capable I too had become of cruelty. It was a very painful realisation, and a difficult one to own, but it was the truth. I was cruel to small children who were innocent. I'm genuinely sorry for my behaviour and take responsibility for the pain and anguish I caused those boys.

Straight after school we went directly to the study room where we talked for a few minutes and then sat down to work. Whether it was that I was extremely tense or had a health problem, I had the greasiest hair imaginable. As a result, I had a routine of first unloading books, organising homework assignments and then I'd head for the washroom where, illegally, I washed my hair, and my one white blouse, every school day, without fail. Afterwards I'd sit on my hunkers, in the yard, in all weathers, drying my hair at the vent of the tumble dryer while trying to learn my Irish. After tea, I tried to complete the remainder of my homework, but often ended up sitting on smelly toilets, with floors flooded with urine, half the night, trying to memorise poetry.

On Saturdays we'd wake up to scrubbing day. At secondary school we'd avoid the morning work as we would be at school, but there was still plenty to be done in the afternoon. We worked with industrial-sized hoovers which encompassed scrubbing brushes and polishers. We pushed, shoved and lifted these extremely heavy implements around the entire orphanage. Starting immediately after breakfast, we were assigned our tasks and were supervised by a lot of staff members. All stairs, landings, toilets, bathrooms, classrooms, and dormitories, were scrubbed, from ceilings to floors. With brillo pads, steel wool, hand-scrubs, deck-scrubs and cloths we worked till we were ready to drop with hunger and tiredness. When we had the place spick and span, and smelling sweetly of turpentine, we reached for the Mansion polish which we applied to the already gleaming floors. Tired as we were, we tried to overcome our feelings of slavery by wrapping rags round our feet and sliding from one side of the room to the other. Occasionally, in our haste we'd crash, sending each other sprawling across the now shiny floors. If the staff caught us, we'd be beaten, or punished by having to do extra work. We felt very resentful and angry about this.

Outside of orphanage life, we participated in the fun and activities with our classmates when we got the chance. But we couldn't mix with them in the normal way. This was because there was absolutely no question of our being allowed out at night, except to go to religious services. I did miss that. I felt, even then, that it was completely abnormal for us to be going out to the school, but not be able to develop relationships with our classmates, like everybody else did. It's as if our classmates sensed this too. They rarely asked us to go out with them and when they did, we simply had to say we weren't allowed, and they accepted this without question. For instance, I remember, at holiday times, some of my classmates would be getting jobs. They'd ask me what I was going to do and I'd just say, I'd probably be staying in the orphanage. They would be telling me about their plans to work for the summer in Lamb's, the local jam-making factory, and where they were going for their holidays when they'd saved enough money. A good many of them didn't come back to school after the holidays and Lamb's factory was definitely frowned upon by the nuns and teachers. One nun belittled the girls who told her they were leaving school to go and work there, even though for some it was a financial necessity.

I knew I would spend only three years at the secondary school though my favourite teacher tried to encourage me to stay on to do my Leaving Certificate. I told her that I couldn't because it would mean staying on at the orphanage another two years, which would take me up to age 18. She seemed understanding about that and I was very deeply touched when she offered me her home address and telephone number and told me to contact her if I needed to. I kept it for about 3 years and I'd feel touched again every time I came across it.

When I reached the age of 16, my term of 'detention' was

completed, and I was free to leave Goldenbridge. I could hardly believe it was finally happening. It was 30 June 1970 and I felt excited as I waited for my mother to collect me. I was dressed in the height of fashion in clothes my mother brought specially for the occasion, and I felt all grown-up. One of the nuns had a brief conversation with my mother and as we descended the steps of the front porch of Goldenbridge, she challenged my mother about an outstanding sum of money which was due for my upkeep. These words immediately deflated my sense of excitement and I was plunged into a state of emotional confusion. I experienced her words as a final indignity.

A torrent of thoughts and feelings assailed me as I walked down the avenue that last time with my mother. While we had a short conversation about the outstanding sum of money, I was so distracted by the thoughts and feelings that overwhelmed me that I didn't pay much heed to her responses. The strongest feeling was one of hurt by the actions of my father. He had, apparently, paid for all four of us right up to the day that the last of my brothers left Goldenbridge for the other orphanages, then ceased paying for me. This seemed proof to me that he didn't care about me and didn't think that I was worth the bother and expense.

I felt angry that he had shamed me. It was bad enough that I had to endure these private thoughts and feelings as I exited Goldenbridge, but I was utterly stung by the fact that he had handed the nuns the ammunition with which they could humiliate me, one last time. The fact that the nuns knew more about my family than I did was extremely threatening. Experience had taught me that any information they possessed reflected adversely on me, in that some of them used the knowledge they had to punish and humiliate me. This was a classic example. I felt as if I had been stabbed. Realising that money was owed for me confirmed in my mind that I deserved to feel ashamed and it validated the nuns' judgement that our parents were bad.

However, I decided not to tell my mother how I was feeling, as we continued down the avenue towards Inchicore village to catch the bus into town. I went away from Goldenbridge forever, leaving it all behind – except for what I took with me in my mind, in my emotions, in my personality and in every other aspect of my being.

CHAPTER TEN

– Why the Cruelty? –

'Pain and suffering sear deeply; they engrave in
indelible letters on the tablets of human memory.'

When I left Goldenbridge I did, indeed, take it with me, and
have spent many years trying not only to overcome its influences on my life but also trying to understand just why the
regime had to be so harsh, so cruel. What on earth led these
adults of the fifties and sixties in Ireland to deal with innocent,
needful children in such an uncaring and destructive way? Why
did so many of us in the religious institutions which were the
organs of the State at the time suffer so badly? How can we
possibly explain it? How did this barbaric system of childcare
come into being? Why did it go unchallenged for so long?

Some explanations I believe can be found in the following
areas: in the history of the Roman Catholic Church; in the
social, religious and political context in Ireland; and in the psychology of the human being involved in such a system.

The Roman Catholic Church

George Ryley Scott in *The History of Corporal Punishment*
outlines the role of corporal punishment in the advancement of
Roman Catholicism throughout Europe. He provides a very
interesting overview of the growth of Christianity and of the
corrupting influence of power. Much of what he has to say is
relevant to the story outlined in this book, and I have found his
work invaluable in my attempt to understand the background

to Goldenbridge. I will attempt here to summarise some of his ideas.

'The whole Christian code of ethics was compiled in accord with barbaric sacrificial ideas', he states. The basis for this is found in the Christian idea of original sin, personal sacrifice, atonement, self-inflicted physical pain and psychological torture, all of which culminated in the sacrifice of Jesus Christ.

Corporal punishment has been inextricably linked to Christianity since its inception, becoming much more heightened around the fourteenth century. Whipping was very common in European convents, and nuns were whipped for failing to observe the regulations of their order. Monks too were whipped for offences such as attempting to kiss or perform indecent acts on young men. Many saints, including St Francis of Assisi, St Anthony of Padua, St Dominic, founder of the Dominican Order of priests, and St Ignatius Loyola, founder of the Jesuits, used flagellation to atone for their sins and to subdue their sexual thoughts and cravings. Flagellation, a form of whipping, was sometimes inflicted by individuals on themselves. It was not always experienced as punishment since it could lead to 'hallucinations, sexual ecstasy and masochistic love of God', according to Scott. Flagellation was seen as a way for monks and nuns to repress their worldly cravings and crucify their own flesh. Fasting was another. Because religious carried out cruel acts on themselves, it followed that what was good for the goose was good for the gander. They prescribed the same medicine for their sinful followers, who could be stripped and publicly whipped for transgressions.

The ultimate transgression was the sin of heresy. Heretics were usually ordinary men and women living Christian lives who disagreed with aspects of Roman Catholic dogma. The Inquisition, set up in the 1330s, aimed to rid the Church of heretics. Courts were established in several European countries and continued to exist for over 500 years until they were finally banned in 1834. All suspected heretics, including women practising astrology and fortune telling, suffered physical torture, sadistic cruelty and continuous persecution until they died at the hands of their tormentors. In the light of such a prolonged frenzy of barbaric cruelty, it was little wonder that the power and influence of the Roman Catholic faith spread with the rapidity of a cyclone.

Cruelty was the hallmark of the Inquisition, and Scott has interesting thoughts on the subject: 'Cruelty, persecution, and humiliation of others, are expressions of the will-to-power.' One of the main reasons for cruelty is the desire to have power and control over others. This desire for power is deeply ingrained in social, religious and political systems and impacts on all institutions of society, for example, schools, orphanages, and the family itself. The staff of Goldenbridge orphanage held power and control over us. They fill Scott's description of those who are 'lifted out of the ordinary rut of life, put in positions of authority, and in the process trample underfoot their fellow human beings.'

Scott also makes the point that cruelty can be a source of enjoyment to those who inflict it. There are people 'to whom the cry, the tear, and the bleeding wound are really a refreshing fountain to still their thirst for blood.' This statement might have come from a war zone. Sadists enjoy punishing others and often deliberately work in institutions where they can inflict pain. Also there is a tendency for those whose work involves inflicting punishment on people to become insensitive and callous towards them. They become so hardened that they forget they are dealing with human beings and deliberately add to the severity of the pain they are inflicting.

It seems to me that what we experienced at Goldenbridge was the tail-end of the historical working out of Church power against heresies, a kind of ingrained attitude on the part of religious in power which encouraged them to stamp out all opposition by whatever means they could, and to assert their own power and that of their religion in domination over any threat. The constant reminders of who we were – the offspring of sinful people – seems to me to underpin the attempt to wipe out any influences our parents might have on us. Everything we were and would become must be controlled by the religious orders and the attitudes they wished to convey. The instinctual, the sexual, the imaginative – anything which hinted at lack of control – had to be stamped out in no uncertain terms. It's as if the system inherited an inquisitorial attitude and operated unconciously with this as its underlying motivation. Punishment was, therefore, good; sensuality was bad. We were even more threatened by our sensuality than 'normal' people because of our backgrounds; therefore, punishment was called for even more strongly.

Ireland: Social, Religious and Political Context

In the nineteenth century poverty was rife in Ireland. The country had been severely marked by cholera epidemics in the early 1800s and the Famine of the 1840s. Workhouses were established to house entire families who had become destitute. Native religious orders of nuns worked in the workhouses and later managed them. They also taught in non fee-paying schools which they had set up for the poor. Poverty, for all sorts of complex reasons, continued to spiral out of control as did criminal activity. Workhouses were considered unsuitable places for children, because there they were exposed to all types of undesirable people.

A bitter rivalry existed between the Churches in Ireland at this time. Ireland was politically controlled by England, and Roman Catholics were denied religious freedoms, while Protestants had both status and wealth. The two denominations distrusted each other's motives and squabbled over the souls of children. The Roman Catholic Cardinal Cullen was extremely passionate and obsessive about the activities of Protestant evangelicals in Ireland. He accused Protestants of seducing poor children, 'to heresy and eternal death'. He vociferously condemned the practice of encouraging poor Catholic widows to hand over their children to Protestants. Soon after they were founded, the Sisters of Mercy were likewise accused by Protestants of 'snatching' orphans of the Protestant tradition.

Cardinal Cullen initiated and zealously supported the work of new religious orders who were founded to combat this threat to Roman Catholicism. There is no doubt that Cardinal Cullen, the clergy, and the religious orders were genuinely concerned about the material and spiritual welfare of the poor. The Cardinal protested at their treatment under the Poor Law Acts, describing such acts as 'barbaric and immoral'. Nevertheless, it would seem that his motivation for encouraging the removing of children from families who were poor or neglectful of them was equally driven by his desire to retain them as Catholics. There is little evidence that the Roman Catholic Church challenged the social and political system which maintained the status quo. Cardinal Cullen, in controlling the work of the Church to the extent that he did, strengthened the role of religious in secular activities.

The 1868 Industrial Schools Act formalised the custody of children of the poor in certified institutions. Financial grants from the state, along with the support of Cardinal Cullen, acted as significant motivation for nuns and brothers to establish such institutions. The main purpose of the grants was to prevent children of the poor becoming criminals and burdens on society. The schools, it was thought, would give useful and honest citizens to the State, as well as providing good souls for heaven, souls who would otherwise have been 'enemies of God and man'. The poor were seen as a huge threat to society, and industrial schools were designed to remove that threat. To be born into poverty was equivalent to being bad, criminal and without morals.

Children were herded into industrial schools under the banner of providing them with shelter, food, training in manual skills and, most importantly, moral formation. However, the real reason for establishing these schools seems to have been more about protecting the wealthy than protecting vulnerable children. With the co-operation and collusion of the religious, the upper classes gained increasingly more control and power over the poor. The Church benefited because it had total control over the moral formation of the lives of the poor. A more hidden objective of the schools was the hope that if children were trained at an early enough age to blind obedience and discipline, society would benefit. The poor would become submissive and respectful to all authority, secular and religious. The long-term aim was that children of the poor would develop into controlled, self-sufficient, honest, decent, hard-working and highly moral adults who would no longer be a burden on society.

How the aims and objectives of industrial schools were achieved is outlined in my account of life in Goldenbridge and, as we saw, much of it was perverse. One particularly cruel method was to break all links between children and parents, because the parents were considered to be bad, unclean, immoral and sometimes evil. One way the links were broken was to ban parents from seeing their children. If they, or their children, did not co-operate fully with the managers of the schools, letters from them could be censored and visits witheld.

Discipline was essential to the smooth running of these institutions, and in cases where children were 'wilfully' disobedient, they were charged with a criminal offence under the rules, and were sent to reformatories. When the children were freed, at 16 years of age, managers were advised to find work for them as far away from their parents as possible.

Structure was a very important part of the school regime and prayer began and ended each day. Every minute of every day was planned. The children were fully occupied at school, involved in industrial training, work, religious duties, moral training and military-like drill exercises. Most of these duties had to be performed in absolute silence and by day's end the children were exhausted.

Punishment was an important feature in all institutions, although enlightened reformers were saying that corporal punishment was not a successful way of maintaining discipline. In 1851, fifteen years before industrial schools were certified in Ireland, Mary Carpenter in her book, *Reformatory Schools for the Children of the Perishing and Dangerous Classes and for Juvenile Offenders,* proved to be well attuned to the thinking and psychology of children. She recommended that institutions should be run on the lines of family type homes, and that the behaviour of teachers towards children should be respectful. She pleaded for the humane treatment of children, arguing that the current moral and punitive attitudes towards them did not encourage the development of a moral sense. She claimed that corporal punishment was demeaning, was not protective of children and had been proved to be counter-productive. She held that it also led to long-term criminal behaviour. This opinion was based on her own experience, the experience of others working with children in institutions, and the experience of Protestant clergy.

The rules and regulations regarding discipline in industrial schools clearly stated that the manager could authorise punishment for misconduct. A punishment book was to be kept, detailing all incidents of 'serious' misconduct, and the punishment meted out. The book was to be made available to inspectors on their visits to the institution. The rules, showing clearly the positive influence of Mary Carpenter, stated that 'managers must remember that the more closely the school is modelled on a principle of judicious family government, the more salutary will be its discipline, and the more effective its moral influence on the children'. The rules, while allowing for punishment, made a somewhat vague distinction between mild and corporal punishment. They did make clear, however, that a less harsh attitude towards children would benefit them and their moral formation.

The kinds of punishment recommended were very clear, but cruel. They included a 'reduction in the quantity and quality of food, confinement in a room or lit cell for not more than three days, and moderate personal correction'. What is of major significance in the light of this summary is the rule that 'no other forms of grave correction be allowed unless approved of by the inspector'. In fact a system of rewards was encouraged by the theorists of the 1800s and was used in some industrial schools. Rewards for good conduct, study and industry were given, but there is no evidence to suggest that the Sisters of Mercy who managed most girls' industrial schools devised any such system of reward. Despite the insight and recommendations of Mary Carpenter, Roman Catholic institutions continued to be managed on highly punitive and moral lines. They housed thousands of children in an atmosphere more suitable for soldiers, quite unlike the respectful family type homes she had envisaged. Clearly she was a woman long, long before her time!

Although the Protestant Churches established industrial schools, they more often pursued an alternative, non-clerical style of management. Staff and management were almost exclusively lay personnel. They were thus less institutionalised and less punishing of the children in their care. By all accounts they seemed generally to be more flexible, merciful and compassionate.

In 1868 when industrial schools were established, Victorian prudery was at its height and led to birching being abandoned in state schools. This goes some way towards explaining the near banning of corporal punishment in the rules and regulations regarding industrial schools. Though some believed that 'the better the flogging the more the learning' others thought it was cruel and degrading. Hand caning replaced flogging, but eventually this too practically disappeared.

Despite the fact that mild punishment was allowed in industrial schools there is strong evidence that as far back as the 1890s managers were breaking the rules by inflicting severe corporal punishment on children. A review of a boys' industrial school in the west of Ireland noted that in 1890 behaviour such as 'disorderly conduct in the playground or talking at night in the dormitory merited a whipping'. Clearly nothing had changed seventy years later when, in the late 1960s, I and others were stripped naked and beaten for the same offence in Goldenbridge.

Despite the fact that some inspectors in the 1890s reported a low incidence of corporal punishment, others felt obliged to censure some managers for their excessive use of the cane. In 1890 an inspector named Rowland Blennerhassett warned managers: 'I must draw the attention of managers seriously to this matter and they must understand that they will be held responsible for any excessive punishment inflicted by any master or official under them.' Five years later, John Fagan, his successor, made several efforts to investigate allegations of brutality made to him by boys in schools run by the Christian Brothers. His efforts were frustrated and he was intimidated by being continuously told that he was on 'dangerous ground'. His solution was to pass the buck back to the boys when he advised them to make their grievances known to the manager.

No changes were made to the rules and regulations in industrial schools until the 1908 Children's Act in England allowed more children to be sent to them, including children under 12 who had committed a crime. This gave the impression that they were milder forms of reformatory schools. It also linked them more closely to the criminal justice system. This link was broken when the Irish government in 1928 transferred responsibility for industrial schools from the Department of Justice to the Department of Education. The rules weren't changed and nothing was done to better the experiences of children in industrial schools.

Meanwhile in England family type homes were operating since the end of the previous century. Serious discussions were taking place in 1935 with regard to the 'rights of the child'. An Adoption Act was introduced in 1939 and professional training for staff began in 1947. As far back as 1873 Stephenson, a Methodist Minister and founder of the National Children's Homes, demanded that child-care workers be trained in order to protect children from 'pious blundering'. Housemothers were expected to be 'competent to take charge of a family group ... of mixed ages and sexes ... In addition to having domestic and other skills they should be able to meet the needs of the child as an individual in a satisfactory personal relationship.'

In 1948 the rights of children were enshrined in the Universal Declaration of Human Rights. Dr T.N. Kelyneck, Medical Director of the National Children's Homes, outlined the rights of children as follows: 'the right to be born in love and honour ... in an environment which will provide for normal development, a right to love, protection, care which will provide health, prevent disease, provide food, shelter and other essentials of home growth ... the right to the affection of parents and their safeguarding by the state ... the right to shielding and protection by the Church ... the right to recreation, companionship with room for self-development, the right to liberty and justice ... and to be safeguarded from neglect, abuse, cruelty, exploitation and every form of injustice

... the right to be treated with the regard due to a child of God'.

In Ireland independence was achieved in 1922 and in 1937 the Irish Constitution was enacted with the aid of Dr John Charles McQuaid, Archbishop of Dublin. It incorporated strong Catholic morals. The Church was a much more experienced political machine than the fledgling government taking on control of the country. The government consulted with the Roman Catholic Church on all matters of health and social policy. The Church saw its role as maintaining the moral standards of the people and the government conceded to its powerful position.

In the 1940s when Cumann na nGaedheal were new to government, Seán McKeown, Minister for Justice, wanted to introduce adoption for what were later described as 'pathetic infants in dreadful industrial schools'. His plan was strongly opposed by Dr McQuaid. Adoption was eventually introduced in the 1950s but with all the hallmarks of Dr McQuaid's intervention. He insisted that Catholic children could only be adopted by Catholic couples. Adoptive parents had to promise on oath that the children would be raised as Catholics, attend Catholic schools and go to Catholic universities. Protestant couples were effectively banned from adopting as were couples of mixed marriages. Meanwhile Dr McQuaid encouraged the transportation of Irish children, many of them secretly, to be adopted by American Catholic couples. It seemed that what mattered most at the end of the day was that Catholics would remain Catholics. Accordingly, young children all over the country lived out their childhood in cruel institutional conditions, while couples of mixed marriages and Protestant couples who were willing to give them loving, permanent homes were denied the possibility of adoption.

The Church had so much power that it had to be placated at all times. The politicians were afraid of a 'belt of a crozier' and Dr McQuaid continued to run the Church as if he were running an ecclesiastical state within the secular state. Meanwhile, it seems politicians were willing to make sacrificial lambs of children of the state, trapped in 'loveless warehouses' like Goldenbridge, where they were afraid of a lot more than the belt of a crozier.

Politicians, like the general public, were influenced by their education in religious run schools in the early decades of twentieth-century Ireland. They allowed themselves to be controlled by the Catholic Church. Nevertheless, there are examples of politicians who had enough moral courage to challenge the power of the Church and take personal responsibility for the political decisions they made.

Dr McQuaid and other bishops controlled the Irish Church in much the same way as Dr Cullen had done in the previous century. They demanded blind obedience from all ranks of society, especially the working class. Nuns continued to be important partners in this system by demanding absolute control and obedience from those in their charge, whether in schools or institutions. The controls imposed in orphanages were related to the fact that the children represented something that was out of the control of religious.

One of the peculiarities of this fine-tuned system was that while we, the children, were punished for the sins of our parents, nuns regularly predicted that we would turn out just the same as our mothers. It was as if the nuns had a personal investment in the cycle of failure. I would suggest that this is one way that they kept their power. If we 'changed our ways', to use the expression of the nuns in Goldenbridge, and became like them in thought, word and deed, they would have considered that they had achieved their goals. But as they clearly were not achieving their aims, they vented their frustration on us children in whose moral formation they had invested so much of themselves. Undoubtedly nuns and other religious considered their function in society to be morally right, and volunteered to uphold certain values. However, religious orders, like political parties, are closed systems, and the members seldom question if what they are doing is appropriate and right. For example, I think it is a strange paradox that a group calling themselves Sisters of Mercy did not show mercy to the children as Jesus did when he said: 'Suffer little children to come unto me for theirs is the kingdom of Heaven.'

Meanwhile, England in the 1940s was paying detailed attention to children living in state institutions. Dr John Bowlby, Anna Freud and others were writing about the acute distress suffered by young children who were put into institutions and separated from people they knew and loved. In 1951, a study carried out by Dr Bowlby on behalf of the World Health Organisation outlined the many debilitating effects of institutional living on children. No attention was paid to this study in Ireland. In fact the fate of children continued to be ignored until 1966 when 'Some of our Children', a report by the London-based study group Tuairim, was published. This study gave a fairly accurate account of life in orphanages and noted a complete lack of understanding of the needs of children. It pinpointed with concern the fact that local authorities did not pay maintenance grants on time, thus imposing extra strains on the system. Commenting on the lack of services for children in care the report stated that, 'provided the child was physically healthy, well clothed, obedient and could speak Irish, Irish officialdom was satisfied'.

In response to this study, the Irish government finally made a decision to pay some attention to the needs of children languishing in Irish industrial schools, or orphanages as they were then called. In 1967, the Minister for Education, Donogh O'Malley, commissioned 'The Reformatory and Industrial Schools Report', also known as the Kennedy Report. It was completed in 1970, the year I left Goldenbridge. Though it was a progressive report, and made many recommendations, most of these were not implemented until the Children's Act of 1991, which came into force in 1996. After all of this time, as Ireland approaches the new millennium, some children in the care of the state continue to live institutional lives in institutional buildings, though hopefully under a much more caring regime.

The Person who Upholds the System

We may ask, what type of person upheld the status quo in Irish orphanages? What was the psychological make-up of the individuals involved, which led them to act in cruel and vicious ways? I mentioned that in the history of Christianity fundamentalist tendencies such as flagellation were seen as a normal function of religious life. Evidence from psychological research in recent years, however, places fundamentalism in the category of addiction. The addictive person, it suggests, is drawn to fundamentalism in religion, and Catholicism of the pre-Vatican II era attracted this type of person.

Of course, not all religious are addictive people. Some are decent and good. Those who are addictive, however, feel threatened by change and will do all in their power to protect the organisation, to keep it the way they've always known it. Religious who misuse religion to feel good about themselves sometimes become obsessive and compulsive. Their behaviour is destructive because, like all addictive people, whether alcoholics or drug abusers, they want to deny that they are vulnerable to making mistakes and to the pain of being real human beings. Instead, they want to have power and control over everybody and everything.

The basic message of Christianity is not to communicate doctrine, beliefs or information but to facilitate a process of wholeness. In religious language this is known as holiness and in my experience there were few signs of this quality in the nuns in Goldenbridge. Patrick M. Arnold, a Jesuit priest, explains in his article 'The Rise of Catholic Fundamentalists' that religious addicts 'rarely mention Jesus Christ or the kinds of moral issues that evidently concerned him'. These issues included orphans, as outlined in the letter from the Apostle James when he asked: 'Does anyone here think he is religious? If he does not control his tongue, his religion is worthless and he deceives himself. What God the Father considers to be pure and genuine religion is this: to take care of orphans and widows in their suffering and to keep oneself from being corrupted by the world.' Those religious who ignored the concerns of Jesus Christ and did not live according to his Gospel teachings, chose instead to live by the dictates of Canon Law which were rigid and controlling.

In my opinion it is not possible to justify the harsh and cruel systems these people inflicted on vulnerable children. If they were living by Gospel values and the moral concerns of Jesus Christ they could not have behaved in the way they did. They are therefore condemned by the very person they professed to follow. To my mind there is no justification for the Sisters of Mercy or any other congregation apportioning blame for the way they operated. In citing the historical context in which they lived, and using as an example what others did in the world outside their institutions, they are not taking responsibility for how they chose to live and behave. As instruments of mercy, it seems to me, they could have chosen to lead the way, in compassion and mercy, so that others in society would have learned from them. They obviously didn't grasp the truth that 'the good news of Jesus Christ is the same yesterday and today and forever'. As a result, those of us who spent our childhood in their institutions suffered dire and long-term consequences.

– BOOK TWO –

THE HEALING PROCESS

Recovering from the Experience

CHAPTER ELEVEN

– Stigmatised! –

'That which does not destroy me,
makes me stronger'

On leaving the orphanage I, like so many who were institutionalised with me, was permeated with a range of attitudes, beliefs
and feelings which controlled my life for many years afterwards. Because we were raised in an environment which was
completely different to that of the family home, we learned
and developed different attitudes, thoughts and feelings about
all sorts of matters. We felt, for example, that we were different from people who were reared by their parents. We were
acutely conscious of this, and some of us thought that other
people could see through us and knew that we were different.
The difficulty this posed was that we felt stigmatised and
ashamed about having come from an orphanage. Some of us
were so sensitive about this that, when anyone asked the simple
question, 'Where are you from?', we heard it in 'quadraphonic
sound'. Not only did I think it an impertinent and rude question to ask, but I sweated with panic as I struggled to find a
reply. Invariably, I agressively asked, 'Did I ask you where you
are from?', then proceeded to verbally attack the unfortunate
person for not minding his or her own business. While I sensed
that people thought my reaction was 'over the top', and even
that I was a little mad, my energy was completely taken up with
trying to protect myself from the secret and shame over my
time in institutional care. Other girls – and boys – also struggled with these types of questions. They would claim to be

from different places, depending on the knowledge they had about the person asking the question. They tailored their answer to the enquirer! For instance, if they knew that the person came from the the north side of Dublin, they would say they were from the opposite side.

In our attempts to deal with this normal, everyday question, we felt as if we were liars and fakes, but we didn't feel we had the option of telling the truth. In Ireland, as indeed elsewhere, it was not unusual for some children to spend time living away from home, in boarding schools for example. It is a fact that some of these children had experiences in common with us. They lived in very structured environments with every minute of their day accounted for. They lived with nuns, brothers or priests and were subjected to punitively strict and moral regimes. But the similarities ended when we left our respective institutions for the last time, to face life in the outside world.

As young adolescents, fresh out of institutions, it was quite a different matter to tell a potential employer that you'd spent your childhood in a boarding school than to say you'd spent it in an orphanage. We were acutely aware of the social prejudices operating in Ireland and knew that no shame was attached to having been educated in boarding school. In fact, having been to boarding school was a source of pride. It brought positive status to the young person who could then wear the badge of honour and respectability. Leaving an orphanage, on the other hand, was a cause for stigmatisation, and we felt we had no status or respectability. So while both groups had the experience of institutionalisation in common, they faced society from opposite ends of the social ladder.

Despite the fact that orphanages were designed to educate us and protect us from the ills of society, we received only minimal education and most of us were illiterate. Lack of education deeply affected every aspect of our lives, leaving us unprepared for and fearful of the world outside the institution. Unlike our boarding school counterparts who got the best of education, we would normally leave school at 16 – if we had got to secondary school at all – because we left the orphanage at that age. After that we had to fend for ourselves. We didn't have the option of attending university and, without the Leaving Certificate or a third level degree or other qualification, we were effectively excluded from work in the civil service, the banks and the professions. With few exceptions, the options available to us were very limited and most of us faced a life of servile work at the lower end of the jobs market. Many girls, on the day they left Goldenbridge, were sent to work as 'live-in' domestics in hospitals run by religious orders. Otherwise, they worked as home-helps for wealthy business families. The few who got jobs as priests' housekeepers were deemed by the rest of us to have climbed up a rung of the social ladder. These, of course, were dead-end jobs with little or no prospect for advancement. They also entailed very long hours of hard labour for little pay.

That Restless Feeling

Many of the girls became conscious of feelings they found difficult to handle. For instance, some noticed that their working lives were reminiscent of routines and conditions in the orphanage. This made them unhappy and unsettled. Sometimes their managers reminded them of abusive adults in Goldenbridge, and they again felt bullied, undermined, abused and controlled. Some were bored, while others were exploited by employers and because they had nowhere to go, felt trapped in their jobs. The most common response to these oppressive work situations was to escape. This entailed uprooting themselves and, often without support or help of any kind, finding new jobs and homes for themselves.

A common feeling that developed among the girls,

whether or not they liked their jobs, was that of always wanting 'to get away'. Perhaps this can be related to the fact that as children they hadn't the freedom to come and go, and as a result felt confined and trapped. Some couldn't tolerate the rules and regulations of their live-in places of employment. Others, as soon as they had settled in new jobs, felt uncomfortable about staying in any particular place, for any length of time, and set about planning their next move.

Some experienced difficulties of another kind, which they now believe is associated with their experience of institutional life. They felt that, however lowly or senior their job was, they were inferior to their co-workers. In an effort to overcome feelings of inadequacy, they worked hard to please and actively sought praise and approval. Some did this by attempting to emulate their co-workers. They copied their mannerisms, behaviour and style of dress. Unlike their co-workers who often looked and felt the best, some of the girls looked the best, but felt the worst. Many have told me that they knew they were not 'real', that they felt like fakes. When they thought that co-workers saw through them, they impulsively left their jobs, often giving different explanations to different people. Some recall the fear of bumping into old work-mates because they couldn't remember which reason they gave them for leaving the job. Besides, they were busy striving for yet another 'fresh start'.

Though they never felt good enough to put themselves forward, some tried to compensate by doing whatever they thought would win them the praise and approval of their employers. When they achieved this, they became fearful that their bosses could see through them and know what they were at. Once again, out of a sense of shame, they impulsively left their jobs. It is clear that in some cases lack of confidence, self-esteem and self-worth contributed to an inability to settle in jobs. This repetitive cycle of uprooting themselves every time they changed jobs did not contribute towards a sense of belonging, which is an important component of feeling secure in the world.

In the course of time a minority of the girls reverted back to the only job they felt confident at: the making of rosary beads. This brought them certain advantages. For instance, they worked the hours that suited them, they didn't have to leave the security of their homes, and they were free of the many anxieties and aggravations of the regular work-place. Last, but not least, they were spared the ordeal of social interaction with work-mates outside of the work situation. As a result, many of them became socially isolated and reclusive.

The small percentage of us who were given the opportunity to attend training courses or receive some secondary school education fared better than average among our group. We found less physically demanding jobs as trainee shop assistants, hair-dressers and office workers. We did, however, suffer the same type of inferiority feelings among our peers. For instance, I recall feeling socially inferior to my work-mates despite the fact that I was better educated than some of them. This did nothing to enhance my self-image. I was somewhat paranoid, certain that they could see through me and that they knew I came from an orphanage.

Unlike young people leaving day or boarding schools, who had the protective environment of a family home to support them, those leaving orphanages had no such haven. This was a huge disadvantage on the practical level, in that, for example, we didn't know where to seek advice when we felt we needed it. Neither had we knowledge of how to obtain financial support, or how to acquire the help of state and voluntary services to sustain us through periods of transition, such as job or home changes, all normal experiences in the journey through life.

Isolation and Loneliness

On an emotional level, living in a non-supportive environment was, to say the least, daunting. Because we didn't have supportive families to turn to when the going got rough, as it often did, we felt all alone in the world. We had no one special to love and care for us and we didn't feel sufficiently attached to anyone, so the world outside of the institution became as cold and uninviting a place as the orphanage had been.

It is a well-known fact that many people become extremely successful despite having no formal education, so I want to emphasise that it was not exclusively this lack which contributed to the maintenance of our attitudes, beliefs and feelings about the world outside of Goldenbridge. The development of personality is influenced by the social, religious and political context in which we are raised. For us, what was of crucial importance to the development of attitude, belief and indeed personality was the lack of positive and life-enhancing experiences common to children raised in family environments. We were deprived of the expectation that we were just as entitled to an education and a successful life as any other citizen of the state. We were conditioned to believe that we hadn't the right to feel good about ourselves, to feel as valuable as the rest of society. We were dumped unceremoniously into the world, frightened, ill equipped and devoid of the life skills we so desperately needed in order to survive.

Social skills are integral to successful living. Those of us raised in institutional care often lack them, because we did not have sufficient opportunities to mix and interact with people, in social settings, outside of the institution. Within a short time of leaving Goldenbridge, I noticed that while in the company of others I found it extremely difficult to relax and feel at ease with them. For instance, going into public places was an ordeal I found difficult to endure. I felt threatened and insisted on positioning myself close to a door from which I could easily escape if the need arose. It wasn't so much that I felt physically unsafe, it was that the close proximity of other people in intimate environments such as restaurants and pubs, made me uncomfortable. I felt as trapped as someone who suffers from claustrophobia.

I had other problems in restaurants which, while not directly related to a lack of social skills, were definitely throwbacks to orphanage life. Food was long associated in my mind with high anxiety and punishment. It never crossed my mind that eating was an important occasion for social interaction and celebration, that it wasn't meant to be the anxiety-provoking situation that it often turned out to be. It didn't help that I had no experience of eating out on formal occasions, and didn't recognise what cutlery to use with which dishes. The attitudes I brought to food and eating meant it was difficult for me to appreciate what others thought were happy occasions.

To illustrate, an old friend recently commented to me that he felt tense and embarrassed when eating out in my company. This is because I tended to check every morsel of food before I dared eat it. On almost every occasion, I found fault with the food and loudly and inappropriately insisted on complaining to no less a person than the manager. My old friend was not the only person to suffer such indignities. Others have pleaded with me to refrain from creating an unpleasant scene in restaurants. I realise now that because food in Goldenbridge was linked in my mind to deprivation and fear, I had developed a phobia in relation to it. Additionally, I also feared that my inability to handle intimate social situations would be apparent and I did all in my power to divert attention from this. What I didn't realise at the time was that, in my efforts to camouflage my anxiety, I was making my friends as uncomfortable and anxious as I felt myself.

We who have been raised in institutions often feel ill at ease eating in the company of others, particularly with people we don't know. This is because we have lived much of our childhood under the constant gaze of authority figures. As a result, we become acutely conscious about being watched. We feel vulnerable, exposed and open to criticism and ridicule while eating in the presence of strangers and friends alike.

The Meaning of Privacy

How we feel about bodily functions impacts on our bodily image. When we have appropriate and healthy experiences with regard to bodily functions, we are likely to feel respect for our bodies and thus have positive images and feelings about them. For example, in the family home, young people are taught that some rooms are common to all, at all times. They also learn that other rooms, because they serve particular functions, are private spaces and are therefore restricted to use at certain times. So family members grant each other space and privacy in relation to bathrooms, study rooms, and personal bedrooms. In addition, family members honour each other's right to close doors, as an indication that they require privacy. It is accepted practice to lock doors while rooms are in use as an extra precaution against accidental or deliberate violations of privacy.

These are the common, unwritten rules of family life that were not accorded to those of us raised in Goldenbridge. In spite of the heavy emphasis always placed on modesty, we were never given space or privacy. Instead we were constantly exposed, collectively and individually, to close supervision, as we carried out intimate bodily functions, regardless of our need for respect and privacy. In carrying out these functions, we lived in a constant state of anxiety and discomfort, fearful that others would comment, criticise or pressurise us into more rapidly completing our toiletries.

Because our needs in these matters had for so long been disregarded, we later tended to develop an extremely negative attitude and over-sensitivity with regard to bodily functions. For instance, some of us didn't appreciate that bathing could serve any purpose other than its purely functional one of cleansing the body. So for a long time I went through the motions of this ritual, regardless of my circumstances, as if I were back in Goldenbridge, where the pressure was to get in and get out as quickly as possible. I didn't know about luxurious items such as bathing oils that contributed towards making bath times the occasions they are meant to be, opportunities for relaxation and respite from the world.

CHAPTER TWELVE

Attitudes to Sexuality

Because of the constant reminders that we were sources of 'temptation', we became shy, ashamed and maybe prudish with regard to exposing certain parts of the body. This extended to issues of sexuality so that some of us experienced discomfort about wearing short skirts, plunging neck-lines and sleeveless outfits. Without doubt it had a negative impact on our femininity and certainly contributed to our inability to enjoy the experiences of being a woman. Unlike children in family home environments, we didn't have a gender balance of adults or older siblings who could enable us to become comfortable with our sexuality. Instead, we lived with a group of women, many of whom had committed themselves to the denial of their sexual needs. They imparted to us the belief that we too should deny our sexual needs and behave as if our bodies were alien to a friendly touch.

As in all social environments where people live together, we imbibed the values of the adults we lived with. In addition, we hadn't been exposed to values other than those of the nuns, and had no way of broadening our value base. In the area of sexuality, for example, I am aware that I began to think, behave and live like the nuns I had known in Goldenbridge. At the same time I was conscious, almost from the moment I left the orphanage, that I did not feel at ease with these values. I wanted to think and behave differently, but I had been conditioned to certain attitudes and it was beyond my capacity to review, alter or change my thinking about sexual matters. I often over-reacted in circumstances which others thought of as normal. For instance, I had great difficulty coping with compliments. I felt only shame and embarrassment and this was exacerbated when I received compliments from men. Because men made me conscious of myself as a sexual being, I found them all the more threatening. I thought they were frightening and sex mad. This thinking was to some extent born out of the experience of having been raised by celibates in a morally charged climate. Some of us more easily absorbed the values of the nuns and couldn't critically evaluate them. I know that it was the fear of pregnancy and my determination never to expose children to orphanage life, that got in the way of my ability to evaluate and accept or reject these values. In my case, the nuns had achieved their aim.

Within a month of leaving Goldenbridge, I had a boyfriend and was acutely aware of my discomfort in his company. Perhaps because he was the son of my boss, I saw him practically every day and spent a lot of time with him. While I liked him, and he was always kind and considerate to me, I found I couldn't relax with him. It was no reflection on him personally; it merely pointed to the fact that I was uncomfortable spending time alone with men.

I think that, even though he knew I had been raised in an orphanage, I couldn't feel real with him because he wasn't part of that world. I was in a state of acute anxiety every time we were together because I was absolutely terrified that he would ask questions about my family and my past. I was also afraid of the sexual demands he might make on me. He was, however, an absolute gentleman, and didn't exert pressure of any description on me. The real problem was that I hadn't the vocabulary or the confidence to just sit and tell him how I really felt. My energy was taken up with trying to pretend to be a normal girl-friend, when I was anything but that. Within two months of leaving Goldenbridge, my life became one big worry as I tried to cope with the anxieties of having a relationship. I decided it had to end.

Perhaps because they were less impressionable, some girls soon after leaving Goldenbridge managed to break free of the values of the nuns. In doing so, they acquired new ones and lived as they saw fit. One of the first choices they made was to dress as they pleased. I recall feeling envious of them as they shopped in stylish boutiques for their feminine and classy look-ing clothes. Even though a few suffered pangs of anxiety about the clothes they wore, they persisted and became confident and sophisticated-looking young women. Others took bigger steps, abandoning rules about sex before marriage, and began sexual relationships. A friend explained how she arrived at her deci-sion. She asked herself a series of questions while in the company of a man. These included: 'Is this normal?', 'Should I just put up with it?' and 'Should I deprive myself?' Having arrived at the conclusion that sex seemed normal and that having sex seemed like having a good time, she enjoyed the experience and felt that she got one over on the nuns. In addi-tion, she felt smug because she knew it was something the nuns would never find out about. There was, however, one throw-back to Goldenbridge. It concerned the love-bite she found the following day. She was disgusted, because it reminded her not of the previous night's sex but of the many bruises she found on her body as a child.

While the reminder of bruising curtailed this girl's desire for love-bites, others felt that the lack of warmth and love in the orphanage had a huge bearing on how they related to others, in particular, to men. As a direct result of this depriva-tion, many actively sought love. A few believed that when a man wanted to sleep with or have sex with them, the man loved them. The meeting of an essential emotional need to be loved by somebody, was therefore the primary motivating factor for a significant number of the girls. Through following this path they inadvertently released themselves from the values they had absorbed from the nuns.

Many of these girls have told me that they tended to confuse sex with love. Despite the consistent nature of their sexual relationships, they lacked confidence with regard to their body image. Although they hated their own bodies and those of men, they went along with sex because they had become accustomed to doing what they were told. They were submissive and it never crossed their minds that they had the option to refuse or protest. For many, not only did sex fail to fulfil the emotional need to be loved, it had the opposite effect of making them feel used, controlled and unloved.

Other girls have related that although they had sexual relationships with men they were very careful to ensure that their boyfriends were not living with the illusion that they loved them. Some girls made sure that the relationships were run very much on their terms, so that they stayed in control of them. To ensure their independence and in an attempt to protect themselves from being hurt, they were determined not to get emotionally involved with men. They did this by never telling the men what they wanted to hear. A few girls found that this helped them keep control of their feelings, so that when boyfriends said, for example, that they wanted to end the relationship, the girls felt free to let them go. As one of them put it, 'I was saying loud and clear: You can't hurt me.' Occasionally this strategy did not work and created more problems than it solved. This was painfully clear in the case of girls who became pregnant and found themselves back where they started, abandoned, frightened, and alone in a cruel and hostile world.

The Pain of Separation

These debilitating dynamics and feelings are not exclusive to people raised in orphanages. However, they are extremely common among this group. The principal reasons for such high incidence is that, in our early lives, we had been subjected to painful separations from those we loved. We felt abandoned and rejected and, at an emotional level at least, were left to fend for ourselves alone. In addition, we had been institutionalised and suffered serious obstacles in our social and emotional development. We lived with hundreds of other children, unlike those raised in the family home who receive the individual attention that all children need to grow and develop. We were deprived of the usual positive experience of childhood, of feeling secure, nurtured and loved. We missed out on being validated by loving parents, siblings and other members of our extended family, including aunts, uncles and grandparents. These are significant losses for children to bear and are thought to be the single most important reason for the high level of distress exhibited by children in these circumstances. While such separations are obviously extremely painful events, it is the lack of opportunity to form new relationships and attachments with loving adults that causes so much damage to later emotional and social development. Children who suffer separation and remain in caring family environments do not suffer damage to their emotional and social development, despite the significant loss of a loving parent. The real difference between the children in both categories is that those who remain in their family have the consistent, uninterrupted care, love and security of the remaining family members around them.

The family provides the secure base from which children can explore the world and to which they can return when they feel upset and frightened. Children can make this outward journey only when they have formed an attachment with someone they have learned to trust and feel safe with. It is through this process that children feel emotionally secure and gradually become independent.

Young children cry, call, follow and display clinging

behaviour. All of these actions are designed to elicit the care of their loved ones, usually their mothers, with whom they tend to form the strongest attachment. It is the subtlety of the interaction between mother and child that indicates the quality of the attachment. So, for example, when carers look into the eyes of a child, they convey much of what they feel for them. As children grow and develop, attachment behaviour such as crying and clinging diminishes.

When children's attachments are broken or lost, most display signs of separation anxiety or dependency. Others give the signal that they are totally self-reliant and don't need or want anybody else. In other words they become detached and mistrustful of other people. Being attached to a significant person is very important to the emotional development of children. This can be appreciated somewhat more when we realise that the quality of the attachments in the early part of childhood determines the outcome of all future relationships that children make. The purpose of long-term role attachments is to enable us to make successful attachments throughout our lives.

Early attachment relationships set the pattern for all relationships in the future, whether they be close friendships, sexual love relationships or those of parenting. It is from this perspective that we can observe the situation of children raised in institutional care. Because their early relationships were disrupted, or lost, they will display more anxiety symptoms and emotional problems than children who feel loved and secure. Because they were removed from all that was familiar and loved by them and placed in the unfamiliar and non-intimate surroundings of an orphanage, where consistent love was non-existent, they are more likely to have difficulties in relationships with peers. They are also less likely to have a special friend to turn to for emotional support and less able to be selective in choosing friends. Research indicates that they are also more prone to a repetition of the inadequate bonding experiences of their childhood.

Obviously, early, close relationships are formed more easily within the basic family unit than in the institutional setting of an orphanage. Those of us who became institutionalised were deprived of the basic means of obtaining security, since we knew nothing of the security of family. We lost out on the sense of belonging and were left feeling that we did not belong to anyone or to any place. In later life we were thrown out into an unfamiliar, family-based world for which we had no map or compass with which to negotiate our way.

CHAPTER THIRTEEN

Living with Families Again

When they left Goldenbridge a few of the girls reconnected with their families with whom they had long since lost contact. These situations often proved disastrous because mothers had in the meantime given birth to siblings which the girls had not been aware of. This caused rifts in relationships. The girls felt that their mothers could have removed them from the institution and brought them home. Rarely was it possible for girls to come to terms with long-held feelings of rejection and abandonment. Others became angry on discovering the personal circumstances of their mothers, in particular, that better contact had not been maintained.

Some girls went to live with their 'host' families who offered them a home. While they tended to have relationship problems similar to those found in any home, a significant number had struggles of a different kind. Those who knew their host families well, having spent holiday periods and weekends with them over a number of years, tended to do well. They adapted to living in the family environments because they trusted and felt secure with the people concerned. Some knew that if circumstances had allowed, they could have lived with the families from earlier in life. Because they knew this, they had a sense of belonging in those families and therefore adapted well to their new way of life.

Occasionally, even with the best will in the world, things did not work out. One girl, in relating what happened in her case, explained that she thought she felt secure in her host family. She realises now that she never quite trusted them. She worried incessantly that by inviting her to live with them, they had a hidden agenda. She couldn't quite believe that they took her at face value and readily accepted her into their home. Because she had suffered trauma in her family of origin, she fully expected to experience a repetition of this in her host family. She lived in fear of not knowing who she could turn to if things went wrong in her host family. Happily, that which she feared didn't happen and she lived with her host family until she married.

Another girl, in retrospect, also realises that she displayed her insecurities in her host family in all sorts of ways. She had an overwhelming desire to feel accepted, have a sense of belonging and not be a burden on them. So she got up before the rest of them, prepared breakfast and went as far as taking it to them in bed. She then rushed around cleaning to save them the effort and work involved in caring for her. Because as a child she had been rejected by her own parents, she couldn't begin to imagine what her host family saw in her. She had always believed that it was her fault that she had been abandoned by her family of origin and as a result didn't like herself. Because of this she came to the conclusion that she didn't deserve any better and was suspicious of the motives of her host family.

Other girls in similar circumstances settled relatively well but at the same time suffered a great deal. Some had difficulties which centred on food. One girl in telling her story realised that it wasn't so much that food was the problem but rather that she felt such a burden on her host family that she wanted to disappear. Within months of leaving Goldenbridge, she had lost two stone in weight. In her efforts to be as little trouble as possible, she ate only food which required little chewing. She wouldn't eat foods such as apples, crackers or cake because they made a mess or caused her to make sounds which would bring other people's attention to her. She was embarrassed about saying that she didn't recognise certain foods and didn't want to eat them because she didn't know what they tasted like.

Others brought institutional habits into their new homes. One girl recounts how, as soon as the last morsel was eaten, she snatched dishes from the table and rushed to the kitchen to wash them. Other times she took the initiative to prepare and cook meals hours in advance of meal times. As was the procedure in Goldenbridge, she apportioned certain amounts of food to each person and left the prepared meals, cold and covered, on the table. The family, although kind in their responses to this behaviour, were made to feel as if they were inefficient and disorganised in their own home.

A few of us who, throughout our time in Goldenbridge, had maintained contact with relatives, went and lived with them. Against all the odds a number of these situations worked out very well and all concerned adjusted to their new circumstances. In the majority of cases, however, things did not work out. My mother, because she had no home of her own, arranged for me to live with her relatives whom I'd known from visiting regularly during my time in Goldenbridge. They were my Aunt Mary, her husband Michael and their four children. They lived in a two-bedroomed flat in the centre of the city. While it was very convenient to live in town where I was close to my brothers and other relatives, living conditions were quite crowded. Because I had spent so much of my life living in over-crowded conditions without physical space and privacy, I wasn't happy in my new home. I had become unaccustomed to family life, and I found it very stressful because I'd forgotten how to behave in a family.

My mother, in the meantime, continued to live full-time at her place of employment where she was rearing the children of her employers. As usual, she continued to visit my brothers in the orphanage in Dominick Street where they still lived. She continued to take them out on Sundays and I very much enjoyed spending time with them on these occasions and at other times when I visited Dominick Street. Although I always felt that the priest in charge didn't like me and didn't approve of them keeping company with me, they seemed to like spending time with me too.

While I was comfortable in my relationship with my brothers, my experience with my mother was different. I had a fantasy that once I was free, our relationship would be a golden one. This proved not to be the case and I was distressed when she frequently disapproved of me – of the style of clothes I wore and the kind of personality I had. Though she continued, as always, to be generous in material ways, I hated the way she criticised me and wanted me to change. I suspected that she didn't like me and this became the most difficult feature of our relationship.

In my head, I convinced myself that she loved me, though my feelings were telling me a different story. I ignored these as it would have been too painful to acknowledge they might be true. My frustration centred around a longing that she would like me, accept me and cherish me as her daughter. Because in my head I pretended we had a good relationship, I shared many of my everyday concerns with her. Her response was always different to what I needed. This annoyed and confused me as inevitably she ended up undermining and criticising me. Though these encounters left me with the impression that she hated me, they never seemed to deter me from going back and trying to get her approval and the love that I so desperately wanted. I recall that during this time, in my attempt to get some emotional warmth, I stole my cousin's teddy bear to comfort and console me at bedtime.

I also wanted to feel close to my aunt and I talked to her about everyday concerns. But a problem quickly emerged. My aunt was very close to my mother, and naturally, as a matter of course would relate to her things I had shared. Though it was not her intention, this often rebounded adversely on me. To defend myself from negative reactions, I decided to share nothing of importance with either of them. My uncle was always a quietly patient and kind man in his dealings with me and I felt I could have more easily shared my concerns with him. Regrettably I never did. This was because I had a bigger investment in trying to get the approval and love of the important women in my life. Feelings evoked in me in the family home environment were confusing.

While I was unhappy and discontented at an emotional level, there were compensations. For instance, my relatives readily welcomed my friends and were not strict about how much time I spent socialising with them away from home. It meant that I could continue to enjoy the freedom of being out of the oppressive and controlling atmosphere of Goldenbridge. On balance, though, I did not feel happy in my new situation. Because I felt stifled in my relationship with my mother and because I couldn't settle in a family environment, I decided it was time to get out. Fast. Within two months of leaving the orphanage, I found I was unable to handle living in a normal environment.

One day a social worker phoned me out of the blue and said she worked for the Sisters of Mercy at Goldenbridge. Initially I was alarmed and told her I didn't want anything to do with her. The reason was that I didn't want any contact with the nuns and didn't want them interfering with my life. She prevailed upon me and we arranged to meet. On the day, I tried to evade her because I reverted back to my former position and didn't want to trust her. However, we did talk and I was relieved because she agreed to help me find a hostel to live in. A few of the other girls who had no host family or family of their own, and had office jobs, lived in hostels around the city. Though the hostels were run on strict lines, the girls seemed happy to live in them. It was on that basis that I decided I wanted to live in one. I had noticed that when I met those girls they seemed happier than I was. I thought that this was because they didn't have to deal with family problems. They were more relaxed than me and I seemed to be the one doing all the moaning. We used to just walk around town and go to the pictures, but we never went to plays at theatres or anything of that kind. Some of them used to go swimming but I wasn't interested. I didn't like the idea of undressing or getting cold and wet, unnecessarily as I saw it. Besides, water, especially cold water, always reminded me of cold baths in Goldenbridge.

Inside myself I knew that it was something about me that made it difficult for me to settle. It wasn't any fault of my aunt or uncle. I had tried to broach the subject with my mother, but she was hostile to the idea to my moving. The social worker reassured me that she would get me a place in a hostel run by the Sisters of Our Lady of Charity and within weeks the social worker honoured her word and took me to visit the hostel. I was impressed with the building, which was anything but institutional. It was warm and comfortable and instinctively I liked the nuns who struck me as genuine and kind in their demeanour. A date was set for me to move in. I was gloriously happy.

CHAPTER FOURTEEN

A Half-way Home

On the day I was to move into the hostel, I finally summoned up the courage and broke the bad news to my mother. A serious row ensued and later than evening, with the help of my supportive twin brother, Michael, who was out for a visit from the orphanage he was soon to leave, I took a taxi to begin my new life. The move caused an estrangement with my mother which lasted for several long months. Within months of leaving Goldenbridge, I had changed my home, ended a relationship, and faced changing jobs. Though I loved my job and liked the people I worked with, I felt confined because I had to work in one room, doing the same thing all day long. I had moved to the opposite side of the city now and this meant it was impractical to commute across the city. So with ambivalent feelings I left. The ambivalence centred around my wanting to stay because I liked the job and the people, but I also experienced relief about getting away from the feeling of being stuck in one place.

My new job was interesting because it was with an international company which had many branches throughout the world. Although I was very much the junior, the company had a policy of treating its staff very well. This policy was reflected in how well senior staff treated a junior such as myself. Though I was still very much the classic girl from Goldenbridge who lacked confidence and self-esteem, the management and staff didn't know I had been raised in an orphanage. That made me feel a little better about myself because I felt less exposed than I had been in my old job. Besides, it helped that my new employers thought I was worth enough to offer me twice the salary I had been earning in my previous job.

Life in the hostel was great. There were about 15 girls, many of them from the country working as civil servants in Dublin. Most of the girls had single rooms and I was upset to find that I had to share a room with a girl who was from the country, though in time my room-mate and I became quite close. The hostel was managed by a nun, who had to be addressed by the title 'Mother'. I thought this was strange and in the beginning I nearly choked every time I used the term. In time, it became easier because I liked her and thought she behaved as a mother ought to.

It was during this time that it dawned on me that from the moment we entered Goldenbridge, I had stopped addressing my mother with her title. Instead, I just began conversations with her without addressing her with either her title or name. I became aware too, that when I talked about her, I referred to her as 'the mother'. I thought it was very odd that I did these things but I didn't know how to explain them to myself. Other people noticed and remarked on it but I never reflected on it very much. I just knew that I couldn't refer to her like children in families referred to their mother.

In the hostel we had plenty of freedom and the nun in charge, who was disciplined and firm, was also very reasonable in her dealings with us. She was aware that I wasn't happy about sharing a room, and I was impressed when she initiated a discussion with me about it. I was extremely touched when she explained that one of her reasons for making this decision was to enable me to settle in and to help me make new friends.

I found it difficult to believe we could be treated so well and with such respect. We paid a fair rent and received very good care in return. The hostel was well managed and we happily co-operated in keeping it clean and tidy. There was no harsh regime and absolutely no violence was directed at us, verbal or otherwise. We had full access to all facilities and we were presented with a thoughtfully prepared hot meal in the evenings. We prepared other meals for ourselves and I soon developed a reputation for making the best scrambled eggs. I was amazed when the nun in charge asked about which foods we liked and endeavoured to provide them. I had never experienced anything like the consideration I was getting and I thrived on it. I felt like something more than a body that needed food, heat and clothing.

There was a youth club in the grounds of the hostel, also run by the nuns, which they encouraged me to attend. I did and liked meeting new people and participating in the many club activities. Some of the girls from Goldenbridge also came to the club and so we had a place where we could meet regularly. This helped because some of them were by now living in digs, where they just rented a room in a family home, but didn't necessarily live as part of the family. The nuns in the convent were friendly and some of them along with seminarians from All Hallows, the priests' training college, also joined in the activities at the club. It was good clean fun and I began to notice that I liked some of the adults around me. These included nuns, some of whom were easy to talk to. I became very fond of a few of them. One nun in particular took a special interest in me, and invested quite a lot of energy and time on me.

Unlike the nuns in Goldenbridge, she and other nuns seemed to like me and expressed affection for me. I found it hard to believe that they really cared for me. Nevertheless, it did make me feel good. It also stirred other feelings, which at the time I was unable to verbalise, and this created a lot of confusion in me. For instance, I noticed that as soon as I was alone, all sorts of anxieties and insecure feelings welled up in me. As a result, I couldn't bear to be alone, and as soon as the nun left me, the good feeling I had left with her and I always felt abandoned again.

Keeping the Agony Alive

No matter how much friendship, concern, understanding and time my kind mentor gave me, it was never enough. However, hard I tried to hold on to the good feelings, I couldn't, and I felt as unloved as ever. This led to a deep and painful longing which nothing and nobody seemed to be able to eradicate. It was like a festering sore in the centre of my emotional being and made me so needy that I ended up hating myself for that. I also hated myself for being so emotionally demanding of her and of others.

There's no doubt in my mind that she experienced me as extremely needy and while I was intelligent enough to know that, I wasn't able to do anything about containing my emotional needs. She was always kind and patient but I thought that my neediness might frighten even her. However, no one was more scared and frightened than myself. I was intensely ashamed and was absolutely terrified of the strength of my feelings. I spent many hours alone in my room, crying my heart out about these kinds of things, but beyond that I didn't know how to control my emotional needs.

Occasionally, my room-mate would find me in a state of abject grief and I began to talk to her about my life in Goldenbridge. She came from a loving and happy family and while she tried to comfort me, I think she just couldn't believe what she was hearing. This was something that I and others girls had noticed since we left Goldenbridge. We had the feeling that some people thought we might be exaggerating in telling them about our past. This made it even more difficult to talk about our lives and we felt that nobody really quite understood. I certainly sensed that some people just went through the motions of listening but didn't heed what I was saying. In retrospect, I think it was less about their not wanting to heed us and much more about their not knowing what to do with the stories they heard.

In their efforts to stop us moaning some people resorted to telling us to 'stop looking for sympathy', to put it all behind us and get on with the rest of our lives. That might have made them feel better but it was terribly painful for us to bear and added to our frustration and pain. I used to scream inside myself that that was easier said than done. We became resentful because, as a friend put it to me recently, 'I didn't want to forget about it and I couldn't get on with my life without getting it out of my system.' Another put it this way: 'It was always in my head and I sensed it wasn't going to go away however much I wanted it to.' Some girls still get what they describe as constant 'flash-backs'. They can never forget it and don't feel that they have any choice in the matter.

I think now that part of other people's reality was that for all sorts of reasons they were not quite able to identify with our experience. This was to some extent clarified in later years by one of my counsellors who has since remarked that even though he heard what I said and would try to show empathy, he realised that, having been reared in a middle class family, he really didn't understand what it was like to have lived in an orphanage. He acknowledged that he hadn't understood the depth of feeling associated with that particular experience. He admitted too that it was as if he was speaking a very different language to me. This may have contributed to some extent to the feeling I had that he had missed the nub of my problem. He also speculated that in his trojan efforts to convey his empathy, he deliberately used similar words to mine, not understanding that in doing so, we had attached very different connotations to them.

Because they found that their friends who had been raised in families didn't appreciate what it was like to live with horrible memories, some girls reminisced about the things that happened, remembering and telling, constantly harking back, keeping the stories alive. Other decided to shut up, say nothing and try to pretend that these things had never happened to them. This to some extent explains why the experiences of people raised in care remained, until recent times, one of the biggest secrets in Irish society.

It didn't help, I suppose, that when we were retelling our stories, we were making what sounded like disparaging remarks about religious people who were still held in very high esteem by most of Irish society, although when we told our stories people sometimes responded by outlining incidents which occurred in their own lives at the hands of religious in day schools. This was, no doubt, their attempt to empathise with us, but they missed the point that we were talking of experiences at a different level.

Another serious obstacle to having our stories validated was that we didn't have the vocabulary at the time to adequately describe the impact of these experiences on our lives. Having acknowledged these difficulties, there were some people, particularly professionals in the psychiatric world, and including religious, who could and did hear what we were saying. Some decent religious who listened to these stories have since told me that they believed what they heard, but didn't know where to go and what to do about it. One told me he feared a Spanish-type Inquisition which would require him to produce convincing evidence. He was in no position to produce such evidence since the only basis from which he would make representations was the horrific story he heard concerning life in a particular orphanage. All he could do was outline the story and indicate that he had no reason to disbelieve it. Another told me that he seriously considered relating to senior clergy a story that he had been told, but the person who told him her story would not agree to co-operate because she didn't feel strong enough to do so at that time. A childcare student of the 1980s told me that as part of his research thesis he wanted to do a comparative study of a group who had been raised in care and a group who had not. He was prevented from doing so by religious managers of several orphanages. In making the point that he now understands why, he was alluding to the stories which came into the public domain in the 1990s.

Several significant events occurred in my life around this time, which to some extent harked back to the past. The first of these landed me in the Mater Hospital for a week. I had been knocked down and fractured my pelvis. It meant that I couldn't walk for a while. Initially, I didn't know whether or not I'd ever be able to walk again. It was quickly confirmed that I would and this was a considerable relief, because I don't think I could have coped with being permanently dependent on others for my physical needs. While in hospital, however, I felt helpless, as I was suddenly back in the care of the Sisters of Mercy. While it was never mentioned that I had been in Goldenbridge, I was forever conscious of the nuns as they efficiently and clinically carried out their business of running the hospital. Early each morning I went through tortures in my head, as a large, stout nun, with habit trailing behind her, rushed into the ward, slid down on her knees and said morning prayers. She reminded me so much of Goldenbridge that I literally closed my eyes and ears to the sight and sound of her. Needless to say, I was very relieved to return to the good care of the nuns at the hostel who patiently looked after me for several months as I struggled around on crutches.

The second event also concerned my health. The problems I had with my teeth in Goldenbridge continued unabated until I had to have several teeth removed, due to serious gum disease. It was shattering to my esteem, poor and all that it was, and I was still only 16 years of age.

The third and most significant event, however, concerned

my mother. She fell in love and decided to re-marry. She took myself and my brothers aside to discuss her plans and I was gloriously happy for her. I was happy for my brothers and myself too. Although as mother and daughter we continued to have problems relating with each other, I had strong fantasies that once again, we could all as a family live happily ever after.

But it soon emerged that we were not part of her future arrangements, and neither my brothers nor I received a formal invitation to her wedding. She obviously felt she couldn't acknowledge publicly that we were her children. In that era public respectability was probably the supreme value, and having other children was therefore difficult to handle. It was easier for her to pretend that we were not her children, which is what she did, apart from telling her new husband. Beyond that, we were to remain a secret as she took on this new family situation. Unfortunately, having made this decision, it was very difficult to undo the situation in later years. However, we still wanted to take some part in the wedding festivities, so my twin, Michael, and I took a bus into town. On arrival, with Michael protectively supporting me, I hobbled on my crutches all the way down the quays to St Michael's and John's Church to see her get married. We were late and just managed to catch a glimpse of her as she entered a car. We had not been invited to the reception, so slowly and sadly we retraced our steps back to our respective homes.

My mentor, and other nuns to a lesser extent, listened as I struggled through these difficult times. It is true to say that much of the significance of these events did not impact on me at the time, to the extent that they would in later years. In the meantime, I focused much of my attention on my relationship with my mentor as I strove to be as important in her life as she was in mine. I know, in retrospect, that the relationship with her was very significant for me not least because she was a nun. I had always secretly wanted to be cared about, nurtured and

loved by the nuns in Goldenbridge. I think this was what motivated me to invest so much of my energy in pursuing the love
of my mentor and to some extent other nuns. I thought that
their love would heal the horrible wounds of rejection which
weighed heavily on my heart. Furthermore, I used to think that
it would prove to me that I was a lovable person, especially in
the eyes of nuns.

CHAPTER FIFTEEN

Addictive Tendencies

It was also around this time that I began regularly to use alcohol and cigarettes, partly because I thought it was the grown-up thing to do, but mostly because they fulfilled a need in me. Some of us from Goldenbridge used to meet older boys from the club and arrange for them to buy alcohol for us. Drinking was against hostel rules, but was relatively harmless in that we rarely got into trouble, although we did drink too much. The hostel was by now very much my safe haven and I was glad that the rules helped contain my desire to drink more than I should. There were, however, occasional lapses.

One bank holiday weekend I and two others from Goldenbridge hitched a lift out of Dublin, as one of them wanted to visit a relative. We got a lift in a van and I had a hunch that the driver was a Protestant clergyman. On arrival at our destination, he told us he was returning in the evening and would give us a lift back home. The girl whose relatives we were visiting bought them a bottle of gin and tonic water. We spent the afternoon drinking but we ran out of tonic. I drank much of the gin neat and it will come as no surprise that as a result I became very, very drunk.

Suddenly it was nearly time to catch our lift, and my friends were concerned that I was too drunk to travel. In desperation, my friends carried me to a shed and hatched a plan to sober me up. Laughing heartily, they had the good sense to warn me of what was to come. I begged, pleaded and threatened to kill them if they carried out their plan, but undaunted they threw several buckets of freezing cold water all over me. It worked and although I was angry, they managed to get me to the road, where our clergyman friend collected us and brought us safely to the convent grounds. He thankfully had the good grace not to refer to my wet and dripping clothes or comment on the smell of gin that permeated his van all the way home.

On waking the next morning, I had a hangover that was so bad I was unable to lift my head off the pillow. During the days immediately afterwards, I continued to smell the gin as it oozed out of the pores of my skin. I felt so depressed that, to this day, I have never allowed gin to pass my lips again.

Throughout this period of my life, one would have been forgiven for thinking that I was fairly 'happy-go-lucky', because at a superficial level, all seemed well. I was content in my job, and enjoyed an active social life mostly provided and paid for by my excellent employers. While I had little contact with my mother, and none with my father, my brothers and I continued to maintain regular contact and I had new as well as old friends. But in the core of my being, all was not as it seemed. There was major discontent and sadness which always came to the surface, I continued to notice, especially whenever I was alone.

At this point in time, addictive substances were not a major issue in my life. In the course of time, though, they became serious issues in the lives of many of the girls raised in Goldenbridge. Of course, addiction is not exclusive to people raised in institutions, but is very prevalent among them because addictive substances go some way towards alleviating bad and uncomfortable feelings that are a result of such an upbringing, appearing to fill physical and emotional gaps or needs not met when we were children. A few of the girls developed problems with gambling, but a greater number did so with substances such as alcohol and drugs. A significant minority of them suffered chronic addictions, some of which continue to this day.

These addictions, as is so common, led to all sorts of additional social problems such as homelessness and in some cases prostitution. For a few, addiction came later in their lives, often long after they were married with children. Sadly some of them, having built and established homes and families of their own, lost everything. Not a few have found themselves back in institutional care, whether as patients in psychiatric hospitals or as prisoners who were prosecuted for breaking the law.

CHAPTER SIXTEEN

Independence

Less than a year after arriving at the hostel, it was suggested by the nuns that I should move into a flat with some girls from the hostel. This I did reluctantly and though I tried hard to be mature about living an independent life, with the best will in the world I found that I couldn't. The truth is I felt dumped out into the world again before I was ready. In the first instance I had been delighted to get out of an institution, but this time round I was reluctant to leave what had become my safe haven.

Other girls had similar experiences when they had to leave places where they were happy to live. Some, however, found that they continually wanted a change of scene and continued to feel that they couldn't settle in any one place. Whatever our preferences, we had other issues to contend with which caused many of us serious worry and concern. These centred around finance and the continued inability of some of us to manage our money. Such problems tended to dominate our lives when we went out on our own trying to live 'independent' lives in rented accommodation.

In common with everyone else in similar situations, we were entirely responsible for ourselves, but the difference was that a significant number of us didn't know how to manage ourselves and these kinds of responsibilities. One girl, in relating how inadequately she had been prepared for life outside institutional care, told me that she just threw all of her bills into the bin. She simply didn't know what to do with them and didn't understand why she was getting them anyway. She really believed that everything was free, as it had been in the institution. Another related that she knew they were bills, and understood they had to be paid. What she didn't realise however was that *she* was expected to pay them. She had for quite some time interpreted them as mere statements of the cost of keeping her and believed that the state would pay them. A few of us, as you can imagine, ended up in serious debt and found ourselves through no fault of our own up before the courts and in some cases homeless.

Illiteracy was a significant factor in the creation and maintenance of some of these problems. Because of this, girls couldn't have or manage bank accounts and this left them vulnerable to finding alternative ways of borrowing money and seeking credit. Sadly, a number of them ended up in the clutches of moneylenders. This put them in the position of always being in serious debt and under the control of people who continued to prey on their vulnerability. To this day, they have no idea that they are paying compound interest, and because they remain illiterate they have no means of escape from this continuing cycle of poverty and stress.

It seems to me that almost without exception the girls who had happy and stable family home lives after they left the orphanage, whether with their own or host families, fared best in this and other areas of life. They became confident about their finances and in the process learned that one of the realities of life is that we have to take responsibility for our own physical needs. There is no doubt in my mind that where the girls were given this opportunity it contributed in very significant ways to helping them enjoy their lives. Most of this group used the opportunities presented to them, by acquiring qualifications in various professional careers. They now live successful independent lives and enjoy, on average, a better standard and quality of life than those who had no support and had to manage on their own.

This to some extent is backed up by my own experience. Because at secondary school I had studied commerce I knew something, at least at a theoretical level, about money. I knew about budgeting and therefore had the knowledge about how to open bank accounts and deal with financial institutions. What I didn't have though was a supportive family environment in which I could learn from the practical experience of participating in managing household bills and the like. Although I learned something of the realities of living in the world while paying rent in the hostel, all food was provided so I didn't learn to shop for food and had no real idea what it cost to feed oneself.

When I moved into a flat, I paid my rent and continued to spend money on clothes, while leaving food and transport costs at the bottom of my list of priorities. This caused all sorts of problems. For instance, on days when I overslept, as I regularly did, and missed my free lift to work, I hadn't the bus fare to get me there. I became the victim of my own stupidity, but that is not the whole story. The reality was that I hated not having someone to look after me. I felt isolated and became depressed. Then, in my efforts to make myself feel better, I spent even more money on clothes, alcohol and cigarettes.

Around this time I became aware that I was experiencing deep resentment towards my flatmates. When I shared flats with girls from the country, for example, I saw that they went home at weekends and came back with all the washing and ironing done. Their parents also helped support them financially and gave them food parcels. Even though my flatmates shared whatever they had with me, I felt like the orphan who always had to fend for myself and depend on myself for survival. This was a problem even when socialising. Because I wasn't able to say to friends that I hadn't enough money to live on, much less for socialising, in my efforts to do what seemed normal I pretended I could. That helped to keep me in the vicious spiral of more worry and continuing financial problems.

You might ponder the question that since I had a mother who had a good reputation with regard to managing money, how come she didn't act as a role model for me? The answer lies in the fact that our relationship continued to be as it had been when I first left Goldenbridge. In some ways it had even deteriorated but certainly I was adamant that I would not give her further reason to criticise me or make me feel any more of a failure than I already did, so I didn't discuss my worries with her on this or any other matter throughout these years.

To add to my insolvency, because I so desperately wanted my mother's approval, I often spent money buying her things that I could ill afford to pay for. She had only to say that she liked an item of clothing for example and I rushed, sometimes, despite her protests, to pay for it. I allowed my emotions to over-ride what I knew logically was the sensible thing to do. This is a problem common to people desperate for parental approval, whether or not they were raised in institutions, but was very common with girls who were raised in Goldenbridge. It was a kind of inverted parenting, where the adult children in these cases gave their parents, usually their mothers, what it was they, the children, really wanted from them, the parents.

A number of the girls had the experience of actually living with their mothers from the time they left Goldenbridge. This worked quite well for a few. Others realised in the course of time that in their efforts to get their mother's approval, they had reverted back to being as subservient as they had been in Goldenbridge. Some have told me of the roles they found themselves playing in their families. These included becoming cleaners and general maids in their own homes. Essentially, they became the mother figure in the most demeaning of ways, while their mother and, often, new siblings became the arrogant and abusive recipients of their services. In their attempts to restore their dignity and pride some left home, only to find themselves returning as visitors to maintain their demeaning and undignified roles. As in my own case, many found that their emotional needs took precedence over their rational thinking and they were caught in a quagmire of confusion. Some, although perfectly aware of these dynamics, have to this day great difficulty in extricating themselves from such abusive relationships. They devoted huge amounts of energy to seeking approval and simply became stuck in this dynamic.

Escape Mechanisms

Within months of moving to a flat, I began dabbling with 'soft' drugs and this, like so many things in my life, brought only temporary relief. An old friend from Goldenbridge was also experimenting with drugs and one day when I visited her, at her family home, she had taken 'speed'. Somewhat alarmed at her behaviour, I took her to the youth club and spoke to a seminarian student about my fear that she may have over-dosed. He brought us both to the Jervis Street Hospital Drug Clinic, where we saw a psychiatrist who referred us to St Brendan's Psychiatric Hospital.

I have little memory of the admission procedure but I recall that they took us in as voluntary patients for 72 hours' observation. We were put into beds almost opposite each other, in a ward packed with old ladies. Our clothes were taken from us and the door of the ward was locked. Nobody spoke to us for the remainder of the evening and next morning, no doubt as a result of the sobering experience of being locked in, I seemed to miraculously recover and wanted to leave. The doctor and nurses worked hard at trying to convince me to stay, but I wore them down and finally they allowed me to sign myself out.

Although I was relieved at that, I felt very misunderstood, and in a way thought that everybody had missed the point of the exercise. I was unable to communicate that what I really wanted was a safe haven from the world and the problems I couldn't cope with. I wanted and needed help with the black depression which had by now enveloped me and contributed to my perception that the world was a cruel, dark and miserable place. Nevertheless, within weeks, I followed in the steps of so many ex-Goldenbridge girls and emigrated to London.

CHAPTER SEVENTEEN

Escape Route – Emigration

With the help of Goldenbridge girls, within 24 hours of arriving in London I had a live-in job as a hotel receptionist. While I was content for a while with my job, personal problems continued to dog me. I was as depressed as ever, despite the fact that I had plenty of boyfriends and made new friends. In my efforts to cope and maintain a semblance of normality, I continued using soft drugs. Naturally, they had to be sought and paid for and one terrible night, I came close to being arrested, but managed, thanks to the fast tube train system, to evade the police.

Soon after, another Goldenbridge friend, and I had problems with the hotel management and left our jobs. In the process we became homeless. We easily found new jobs with the Gas Board, and a hostel which we happily moved into. On day one, I was caught breaking the no smoking rule, and this instantly made us homeless again. We had to find a flat, fast.

While walking around London, in the early evening, we caught the attention of a Scottish man who offered to help. Within minutes, we were driven by taxi to a part of London we didn't know. Thankfully, the taxi driver was suspicious of the man and alerted the police. Meanwhile, my friend and I were scared when the Scottish man, on entering the house, told us that the electricity was cut off. He brought us to a room where an Indian man was resting in bed. He whispered to him and without a word to us, walked out the front door, locking it behind him.

The Indian man ignored us and we, exhausted from the

day, somehow climbed upstairs, where we found a vacant room with mattresses on the floor. We quickly barricaded the door with all of the furniture we could find and fell asleep. Then we heard the raps on the door and men's voices shouting, 'Police, Police! Open the door.' We ignored them, thinking they were men our Scottish 'friend' had brought back to the house. The police threatened to break down the door and we told them to go ahead because under no circumstances were we going to open it voluntarily. Finally, they smashed the door, passed in their ID cards and we were saved. It was truly a terrifying and humiliating ordeal as the police berated us for our naïvety in falling for the man's ploy.

It would be easy to agree with the police and put this episode down to naïvety. The reality, however, was not that we were stupid but that we were homeless and ignorant about how to get the help we needed to find a new home. We were doing our best to survive in a country we didn't know and in these circumstances felt that we were required to take risks we might not in other circumstances have taken.

I had left Ireland for several reasons, chief amongst which was the feeling that I didn't belong to anyone, anything or anywhere. I was also sick and tired of being asked where I came from and who I was. In common with hundreds of others who were raised in orphanages, I was ashamed of my past and did all in my power to hide it. England was a useful place to evade these issues. It was less parochial. People were happy enough to know which country you came from, and leave it at that. For that reason alone, it became the safe haven of thousands of orphans who couldn't bear the daily pressures that Irish society put on them. We were constantly confronted with our lack of roots and identity. This was extremely painful in a society that laid so much emphasis on one's family pedigree, place of birth, and religious persuasion. These were the barometers by which individuals, families and groups were acceptable or not. There was, as far as we were concerned, little space or attention available to those of us who didn't fit into the stereotypes demanded by the status quo.

While emigration brought us respite from this type of problem, it brought its own struggles in that some of us felt that we did not belong in England. Those of us who were susceptible to feeling easily hurt and rejected, often experienced imagined prejudice. For example, when things didn't go well, I thought it was because I was Irish. Partly in protest, I returned to live in Ireland, to face the demons of my past.

CHAPTER EIGHTEEN

Patterns of Disintegration

Many of us who were raised in Goldenbridge felt a desire to get back at society and we found all sorts of ways to make others aware of our grievances. A few took to shop-lifting. This served different purposes for different people. For instance, some took what they thought was their right to take, without paying for it. In retrospect they would say that they were trying to fulfil emotional as well as physical needs, and it was often resentment about not having the money to survive that drove them to steal in the first instance.

Some in their efforts to protest did so in self-destructive and negative ways such as self-mutilation and attempted suicides. Others 'acted out' their anger on other members of society. They held that whatever they did to others was never going to be as bad as what had been done to them in the past. A few, in carrying out their protest, realised that their illegal behaviour might land them back into institutional care. They took that risk because, as one person explained, she wanted to 'bleed them dry'.

Not all our protest was negative. Some found positive and useful ways of conveying to society what they wanted to say. For instance, several wrote autobiographies which gave them the satisfaction of telling their story. A small minority, including the singer Sharon Murphy, used their talents to write touching but powerful songs, such as 'Sister of fear' and 'Who are you for?' to record their protest. This has helped them to heal and recover some of their lost dignity, as well as contributing to their sense of individual identity.

Soon after my return to Ireland my life took a turn for the better. I got a job as a telephonist in the telephone exchange, subject to getting through the training and tests. Our trainer endeavoured to get me successfully through the training phase. No one was more pleased that she when I did and I was extremely touched when she sent me a congratulations card. I felt for a while as if I had truly joined the human race. I was on top of the world as, finally, I had some semblance of a decent and respectable identity. I was no longer just a nobody who had been raised in an orphanage. I was a somebody, a real Irish civil servant.

My first day as a fully fledged telephonist got off to a bad start. I should have been on duty at 8.00am but awoke at 12 noon. In an absolute panic I rushed out to the phone not knowing what I was going to say when I got through. Although I was prone to oversleeping because of depression, I just couldn't believe it had happened on this day above all days. It was my good fortune that my friend was the duty supervisor and she smoothed the path for me. I was so very grateful for that because I could have blown what was my chance to start, yet again, a new life.

Life in the exchange however was no bed of roses. Some of its rules reminded me of Goldenbridge. The supervisors, with some exceptions, were strict and because they often had to mark me late, I was always anxious in case I'd lose my job as a result. When they didn't 'let me off', feelings of strong resentment and victimisation built up inside of me. Like Goldenbridge, it didn't help that I thought some people were treated on more favour-able terms than others. I lived in the hope that they would make allowances for me, so that I could rest assured my job was safe. They didn't and I hated them for that.

In the meantime, I attended night classes to study psychol-ogy and writing. I studied psychology because I was interested in how people ticked and thought I might learn something about how to deal with my own problems in the process. While I didn't sit formal exams, it dawned on me that I liked learning. I was stimulated by it and became more confident. I noticed too that my vocabulary improved and that I was more easily understood. For these reasons, during my year at the telephone exchange I decided to study some subjects at Leaving Certificate level.

I left the exchange and returned to the Sisters of Charity, who allowed me to live in the hostel that had once been my haven. They did this because they supported my decision to return to school as a full-time student to complete the Leaving Certificate. Within days, I enrolled at Ballymun Comprehensive School and got a part-time job to maintain myself. As in the past I had difficulty with Irish, but a teacher friend from the club days, and her mother patiently tutored me in both written and oral Irish. Irish however proved to be less of a threat to the outcome of my studies than did depression. Episodes continued unabated and in my attempt to survive, I sought the help of the school counsellor. On completion of my studies, it was time once again to leave the 'safe haven' of the hostel, but this was somewhat eased by the good news that I had passed my Leaving Certificate with flying colours.

Depression and Dependency

Now all seemed well. With a Leaving Certificate more work opportunities were available to me, and I was delighted when I was offered a job as secretary in the new Donahies Community School. Eagerly I set about finding a new flat and attempted to live an independent life. But as on previous occasions, I felt emotionally isolated and alone. I maintained contact with the school counsellor and, as in the past, he did his best to support me. Because he was supportive and caring, the old patterns of dependency and neediness which had caused me so much pain in the past, re-emerged. I grew to hate myself intensely. I hated the feeling of weakness and shame but, above all, the loss of dignity which my neediness engendered in me. Not only did I hate myself. I became angry and resentful at every human being, without exception. This was because I thought they had the power to evoke these emotions in me.

The counsellor suggested I should seek more innovative help than he could provide and I went to England to a workshop organised by Dr Frank Lake, a psychiatrist and clergyman. Dr Lake proved to be an angel. He accepted me unconditionally and managed to convince me I was not as bad or as mad as I had begun to believe. Given my story he, as a professional, thought my depression was normal. Not only did he understand its depth, he was able to give me an explanation for all the horrible feelings I had for so long being living with.

I returned from England full of insight and warmth. I thought I would never experience depression as bad again since I now understood what it was and what had caused it. For the first time, I felt safe and secure in the knowledge that with the right help my future could be brighter. I had the feeling that I could recover and cope better with my life's circumstances. I managed to hold on to and maintain good feelings for considerably longer than usual, and I was delighted when I observed this.

Dr Lake was a spiritual man. The theoretical basis for his work lay in the parallels and similarities between the sufferings of Christ as a man and that of the rest of humanity. Given that I had from a very early age compared the experiences of Jesus as a child with our lives as children in Goldenbridge, I was intrigued. I had, in addition, formed opinions about the relationship between God and his suffering son Jesus, and the role of parents in the suffering of adult children. For these reasons I was delighted to find an intellectual outlet and basis for my ideas.

My thinking centred to some extent on the issue of trust,

or rather mistrust. God and fathers, as far as I was concerned, were the one species, and neither was to be trusted. They were just like my father, exerting huge influence, yet invisible. They were unreliable and made promises which they didn't keep. By the time I reached Dr Lake, I was of the opinion that men expected women and children to love, honour, obey and some-times even adore them as if they were indeed gods.

Dr Lake showed me that fear played a significant role in contributing to my anger and my mistrust of others, particu-larly men and male religious. Because men were of superior strength to me, I felt vulnerable, and as a result deeply resentful towards them. These feelings, I realised, were reminiscent of how I had always felt as a child. In Goldenbridge because people were bigger than us, it seemed they could do what they liked with us.

I was also phobic about violence and despite the fact that most violence we suffered was at the hands of women, I was not as an adult too concerned about them because I figured I had the strength to fight them. In hindsight, I discovered that I had transferred a considerable amount of my fear and anger of women onto men. This, I suspect, was because they were bigger and more powerful and could therefore, as I perceived, annihilate me.

Within months of my return from the workshop two inci-dents occurred which in different ways very nearly did annihilate me. The first concerned my father whom I hadn't seen or heard from for many years. Perhaps because he was very ill, he made contact with my brothers. In the course of their conversation when they visited him in hospital he sud-denly made the comment, 'There was a girl, wasn't there?' They confirmed my existence and Michael, my twin, while knowing it would be painful for me to hear this, reluctantly told me because he thought I had the right to know that my father was ill, in case I wished to visit him.

I was devastated by what I heard. I thought, not only had my father literally forgotten that I existed, but he obviously had no idea and didn't give a damn about all we had suffered because of him. I was furious, and did consider confronting him, but decided against it. I thought that because I was furious and felt so rejected, I might lose my temper, and say or do things that I would deeply regret. He died soon afterwards, and although rationally I understood that his illness may have led to his forgetting of me, I couldn't help feeling that it didn't stop him remembering his sons. To this day, I still feel sad when I think about this. Even though I didn't have the emotional capacity to cope with it, I think now that I made the wrong decision in not facing him with his lack of responsibility and the many other painful ways he impacted not just on my life but also on the lives of my brothers.

The rejection by my father re-activated many of the negative feelings I held about men. I reverted back to my old pattern of thinking and feeling – that I was bad and unlovable. But I did manage to hold on to the fact that I had known some positive experiences too. I was fairly stuck, however, in the memories of my father's rejections. Once again I more actively reflected upon the terrible experiences of my childhood. In fact I lived as if 'they' still had the power to control and hurt me. For some years I had suffered regular dreams and nightmares about the nuns and staff at Goldenbridge. There were constant sounds in my head, of children screaming and crying as they were battered. These terrible thoughts and feelings brought me to the brink of suicide more times than I care to remember. I was so desperate to avoid any more emotional pain that I planned many times to end it all. My intense fear of men in white coats, with the power to lock me up in an institution and have power over my life, saved me in the end. That didn't stop me berating myself for being so gutless that I couldn't even kill myself.

The decision about whether or not I would continue to live was, however, soon to be taken out of my control. I was involved in a serious road traffic accident, sustained severe physical injuries and was hospitalised. I awoke from a drug-induced stupor, having undergone several operations, to discover that I had nearly died. I was horrified at being alive.

Though I was surrounded by flowers I felt as alone and isolated as ever I had been. Depression continued unabated and I felt helpless and vulnerable when I found myself unable to move and therefore entirely at the mercy of others again. I felt abjectly guilty about my secret desire to die while everybody around me invested so much energy in keeping me alive and getting me well. I tried desperately not to burden my friends and brothers any more than was necessary and it didn't occur to me that I could have asked to speak to someone other than them. As I reluctantly recovered, I realised I wouldn't be able to fend for myself for some time. Although I was being paid, I couldn't work and I saw no point in renting a flat I couldn't live in. I valued my independence fiercely and the worry was, who would look after me and where would I live? As the time of discharge approached, nobody broached the question. It was as if it were as much a taboo subject for everyone else as it was for me. With only days to go, a psychologist friend raised the issue and offered to provide all that I needed at this extremely difficult time of my life.

Throughout the long months in hospital and into the following year I had a lot of time to think. Much of this thinking centred around trying to make sense of why I had survived. In my efforts to find an explanation, I wrote to Dr Lake. His wife responded and told me of his death. I was shocked by the loss of my good friend. In despair, I renewed contact with my school counsellor who recommended a psychiatrist. I was treated with anti-depressants and tranquillisers which didn't alter how I felt about anything.

I struggled on, giving an outward impression to all around me that I was recovering well and that I was happy to be alive. The accident had taken its toll on me and now in my head I was hearing more than the sound of screaming children. I was hearing the sound of my own screams and shattering glass as the cars collided. Nightmares continued and frankly I was a physical and emotional wreck. Again life was unbearable and I was referred to a second psychiatrist who again treated me with medication and later with several hospital admissions for more intensive treatment.

Many of the other girls also came to the attention of the psychiatric services and received similar medical treatment. Unfortunately what started out as emotional problems for them, as for me, degenerated into psychiatric illness and the emotional problems were no longer the focus of the treatment they received. Sadly, many of these women spent much of their adult lives on medication and became enmeshed in the 'revolving door' system of institutionalised psychiatric care. Some continue to do so, while others who couldn't see the point in continuing to suffer, ended it all, by suicide.

All through this period, although my outer life was punctuated with achievements, secrets continued to be an integral part of my life and brought me close to disintegration. Despite this, I continued working hard at trying to become a 'somebody'. I always believed that education was my ticket to freedom and I now actively pursued it. I had for some time worked by day and studied by night, which culminated in my becoming a teacher. While I was willing to face the strains and stresses of such a demanding workload, I had not bargained on coping with an addiction to prescribed medication as well.

Throughout my studies, two friends supported me without any knowledge of my ongoing problems with severe depression. Still, I often wondered what they thought, when every Sunday they phoned early in the morning to rouse me to prepare for our tutorials. In the afternoons they arrived to find me, having returned to my bed, knocked out and fast asleep. If it were not for the patience of these great and loyal friends, Frances and Jennifer, I would not have achieved my goals.

Drug dependency, for me, was similar in many ways to my dependency on the significant people in my life. While prescribed drugs are designed to alleviate the symptoms of illness, I had always hoped that the significant people in my life would have the same effect. I noticed that drug dependency and addiction brought about the same kinds of feelings as did dependency on particular people.

CHAPTER NINETEEN

Who Am I, After All?

Relations with my mother during this period were ambivalent, to say the least. Following her marriage she decided not to tell her new family of step-children that my brothers and I were her children. This seriously affected my sense of identity. Not only was I struggling to keep my past a secret, I now faced the added burden that my very existence, and that of my brothers, was to become the primary secret to which all the other secrets were tethered. This added further to my already confused and distorted sense of identity. For instance, I didn't know what role I should play with regard to my mother, her husband and her new family of step-children. She gave me no guidance about who I should pretend to be. When we met people she knew, she sometimes introduced me as a friend, while on other occasions she introduced me as her niece. She still found it difficult to resolve this issue in her own mind. I never knew what criteria she used to decide who I was to her in these situations. I could no longer openly say I was my mother's daughter. However, in my efforts to pretend that I belonged to someone and especially to feel part of a real family, I resisted facing up to the reality of the situation and visited her every week.

I liked my step-family. I particularly liked my step-father, the only member of the step-family who knew the truth of our relationship to our mother. He was a kind and decent husband to my mother and, I suspected, a very sensitive man. He once took what I considered to be a huge risk and introduced me to a friend of his as his daughter. To say that I was deeply touched is an understatement and I told him how happy I felt about it. He responded that he didn't see any good reason why he should do otherwise, since he was proud to have me as his daughter.

Because I was a secret in my step-family's life and felt like a ghost who came in and out of my mother's life, socialising with our step-family was always a considerable strain for me. While we chatted and enjoyed drinks in local pubs, problems arose when my brothers and I relaxed sufficiently to 'slip up'. We would forget ourselves and speak about incidents in our childhood which alluded to us as our mother's children or as having been raised in orphanages. The 'slip-ups' were invariably met with kicks, prods or pinches from my mother and we were forced into silence. Many times I felt like blowing the lid off these secrets. I persisted in maintaining control because, as with all significant people in my life, I thought my sanity depended on maintaining my mother's approval. I also had the illusion that one day she would acknowledge my right to my identity as her daughter. Deep in my soul I hoped she would set us all free from these secrets. She never did.

The knowledge I gained through study that everybody goes through an identity crisis helped me to come to terms with some of these issues. I no longer felt as isolated, thinking I was the only one experiencing this kind of struggle. In the course of my studies I learned that people who form a healthy sense of identity have a clear understanding of who they are in relation to other people. They reach a conclusion about which values and standards they choose to live by. They set appropriate goals for themselves and their lives, which go some way towards giving them a sense of purpose in society and some meaning to their lives. I learned that to develop an identity, everybody has to go through a psycho-social development process that begins at infancy and continues into adulthood. In going through each of these stages, we are all faced with challenges during which a life-task has to be accomplished.

In going through stages 1 to 4, which begin at infancy and continue until adolescence, the most important emotional tasks we need to accomplish are trust in others, trust in the environment in which we live and trust and confidence in our abilities and in ourselves. Ideally, we achieve this through the consistent discovery that in all the age groups we can achieve tasks appropriate to our age. Failure to achieve these tasks damages our potential for the successful formation of our identity. One girl I knew, in alluding to her failure to achieve her potential, made the point that because she had not received a basic education while in the orphanage, she felt 'about 10 years behind where I should be in relation to everything. I never had any encouragement to dream beyond being a nobody.' This statement indicates the adverse effects that can follow when we do not succeed in accomplishing the tasks appropriate to our age and stage of psycho-social development.

Another girl describes the marks institutional care left on her as follows: 'I felt lost. I think we are starting off as if we were at day one again, because we have to learn all about emotions, feelings and how to express ourselves, so really coming out of an institution is like being reborn.' Some of the girls came to realise and understand that because they didn't have the opportunity to learn to trust others and feel safe and secure in the orphanage, this seriously hampered their chances to accomplish and achieve in the outside world. In fact, it contributed in major ways to the lack of physical and emotional resources available to them to succeed in the world. Instead of leaving the orphanage with a strong and positive sense of who they were, they left with little or no self-esteem, a lack of purpose and heavy feelings of dependency, guilt and shame.

Stages 5 to 8 of our search for identity occurs after adolescence and it is during these stages that we ponder important questions about who we are and what place we are likely to carve for ourselves in society. It is at this point that issues which were unresolved in the four earlier life stages re-emerge with renewed force. One researcher, while trying to convey what it was like, explained, 'One had the power of the adult but the emotions of the child.' Speaking for myself, I can fully identify with this statement because that is exactly how I felt for many years after leaving Goldenbridge.

Many of the other girls suffered similar trauma. A common catalyst for a number of them was the birth of their first child. While bonding with their child many wondered how it had been possible for their own mothers to give them away or abandon them. Some understood the social and religious circumstances and pressures under which their mothers laboured, but they found it extremely difficult to understand this from an emotional perspective. This is partly because the girls, as mothers, simply couldn't contemplate parting with their own new-born children with whom they had just bonded. Their abhorrence at such an idea is as old as civilisation and is reflected in the bible in the cry of the prophet Isaiah, 'Can a mother forget her baby or a woman the child within her womb?'

Once these feelings were evoked the girls had to discover who they were both for their own benefit and for the benefit of their children. As one of them put it, 'When I became a mother, it was like I wanted a mother too.' All felt that their children had, at the very least, the right to know the identity of their grandparents, aunts, uncles, and cousins. They were entitled to these relationships, and the girls didn't want their children to be deprived of them, like they had been.

Not knowing who they were themselves, and starting out on a journey to discover their identity, was like trying to read a map while blindfolded. It was at this point that many realised they had always been rootless and had no foundation stone on which to begin the search for the identity of their parents. They felt angry and cheated of their birth-right, their human right to know from where and from whom they had come. Some of them, on leaving Goldenbridge, hadn't been given a birth certificate, and they were soon to discover that no such document existed in their name. This was devastating for them because not only did they *feel* they hadn't an identity but officialdom confirmed this reality. Others, on procuring their birth certificate, found that the names on them were false. Naturally, they too were devastated because effectively all hope of ever discovering the true identity of their parents was lost forever.

For the lucky ones whose parents' names were accurately recorded, some managed to trace both parents, but more commonly only mothers were traced. Often these women had emigrated to begin new lives and had started new families. Many mothers, because they had not revealed the existence of their previous children to partners and new families, didn't want to renew contact. While some girls accepted this philosophically, others resented it very deeply, sometimes going as far as carrying out their threat to reveal their existence to their mother's new family. Often, after time-consuming and expensive searches, they found themselves in worse positions than when they started, rejected and abandoned for the second time. Understandably, they were plunged into depression and extreme anger from which some have never fully recovered.

CHAPTER TWENTY

Healing – a Personal Journey

Shared experience, shared inheritance, shared emotions can help us identify with others and understand what we are all going through. But I suppose a point comes when we must take flight for ourselves, embark on our own very personal journey, a journey which truly establishes the uniqueness of ourselves as individuals. The following is a glimpse of my personal journey and I include it here to share just one story of survival of Goldenbridge, one way of coming to terms with the legacy of that type of institutionalised upbringing. Other people grew their sense of self-worth and their strength in different ways. My story may help people understand the long struggle involved in shedding the heritage offered by a confused, dysfunctional family situation and a cold, impersonal, cruel institution.

Because of continuing addiction, depression and other severe stresses, I decided to follow up on the suggestion of Dr Lake that I should seek the help of a particular counsellor whom he had recommended. The reason I hadn't done so to date was that I couldn't afford it. The time had come now though and whether or not I could afford it, I knew I had reached the limit of my endurance. It was clear I needed help and, like a tiger fighting for its life, I made the decision. I would fight to preserve my life. In doing so, I was prepared to go hungry, because I had long realised that life without peace of mind was not worth living. Education continued nevertheless to be a priority and I sought work in the ambience of a new university. While I enjoyed the job immensely, much of the work was technical and I had difficulty maintaining concentration. Not only was I struggling with my emotions but, in addition, I continued to suffer severe pain as a result of physical injuries received in the road accident. For the first time ever, I had neither the physical nor mental stamina to withstand the stresses and strains of my life.

The first issue which my therapist addressed was my addiction to drugs. She referred me to a homeopathic doctor and in a short time they weaned me off my dependency on them. Because I was eager and willing to recover from life's experiences, I worked hard at developing a good working relationship with the therapist. All went well for the first few months and, once again, I was 'in love' with the new significant person in my life. While it was difficult and painful to deal with the emotional issues raised in therapy, I endured it because I was desperate to get well and find lasting peace of mind.

Within months, however, old patterns broke through and I became as demanding as I had ever been in my life. Naturally, we discussed this and its impact on the relationship. While I understood that my behaviour was not helpful to me and was destructive to the working relationship, I wanted the therapist to sort it out since clearly I didn't have a clue how to behave in a so-called 'real relationship'. What this amounted to was my inability to respect other people's boundaries. I was forever impinging on my therapist's private space and life. This upset her deeply. I didn't appreciate that other people's feelings, and particularly my therapist's feelings, were as valid as mine.

It didn't help that although I deeply appreciated the love and support of my therapist, I expressed my anger at having to pay for it. I felt as though I was prostituting myself and wondered out loud what would happen when I could not afford to pay for it. This caused me great anxiety and it seemed that the help I received was conditional on my ability to pay for it. I also became aware of the fact that others had the power to accept or reject me and I deeply resented that too. Moreover, I noticed that I always seemed to be the loser in this game of poker and frankly I was thoroughly fed up with it. This is the baggage that I brought to the therapist and it would be hard to deny that I was a thorny client.

Nevertheless, my therapist was patient and persisted in her work with me. In the process of relating I got a lot of insight into why I was so lacking in trust, self-confidence and self-esteem. Episodes of depression were significantly reduced and I learned a great deal about respecting my right to acceptance, respect, esteem and validation. I also learned that this was a reciprocal process and that others had the right not to be rejected, abused and invalidated by me. On a practical level this was news to me. While I believed that everybody should be treated well, my behaviour around these issues was not congruent with my beliefs. For instance, I constantly criticised, judged and abused others. I learned that I was capable of doing unto others that which I didn't like done unto myself. Therapy, I decided, was the best university in the world.

Despite my faults and failings my therapist worked hard to encourage me to accept myself. She taught me that it was a fruitless exercise to try to force others to love and accept me. I had to learn that they either would or wouldn't of their own volition. This was hard to swallow. It meant I had to let go of my efforts to control other people. In essence, my therapist was teaching me to take responsibility for myself, my feelings and my life. I absolutely resisted this. What I really wanted was to hold on to my grudges, resentment, anger and fury. I feared that if I let go of them, all who had hurt, abused and rejected me in the past, would be let off the hook in one fell swoop. That, I was determined, would not happen. I particularly wanted those who hurt me and all the other children in Goldenbridge to be severely punished. I believed that if they were, we would all instantly become free of the scars we had suffered. My therapist tried hard to convince me of the irrational basis of this thinking and pointed out that I was the only person in the equation who was suffering. While I understood and could relate to what she said, I was adamant that I would not 'let them away with it'. Frankly, I thought what they had done was unforgivable and I determined to fight them to the bitter end.

While I was free to stubbornly continue to hold on to my feelings about this and other matters, I didn't easily adapt to letting go of my need to be at the centre of my therapist's universe. I insisted she love me exclusively above all else. I sought a commitment from her that she would never reject me. I was furious when she refused and I 'acted out' my anger, becoming extremely aggressive and deliberately smashing a door with my bare hands. After years of hard work, my therapist finally made the judgement that I had become unmanageable, that the relationship was untenable and that she could no longer work with me. I was, it seemed, back to square one.

My reaction to the news was ambivalent. On the one hand, the sense of relief was enormous, relief from the struggle of the pain of failure. It was clear for some time that someone or something had to give. I hadn't the strength or courage to end it. It is no exaggeration to say that I felt as dependent on her as I did on the air that I breathed. On the other hand, I experienced the break as the most cruel and most awful rejection of my life. Blaming her for all that went wrong, I hated her for letting me down. Then a miracle occurred.

Emille and Margaret, very good friends for a number of years, were as ever there to support me and I sobbed my way through this horrendous time. I fully expected to crack up and have a nervous breakdown. As I lay on my bed I suddenly felt a tap on my shoulder and a voice saying, 'There's no need to worry; all will be well.' The words alone, I thought afterwards, might have come from wishful thinking, but no one can convince me that I was not touched by something like an angel that night. Why I am so sure of this is that I did feel the touch, the voice was unfamiliar, and the calmness I felt was an utterly new experience. I turned to my friends and told them that it was definitely safe to leave me on my own. I was convinced that I would keep my sanity and would not commit suicide as I'd feared. The only fear remaining was how I would feel the next morning. I awoke to the same calmness and the sense that all was well. Something within me was finally laid to rest.

Although the ending of this relationship remained painful, other aspects of my life had over a period of years been moving in a positive direction. During the years of counselling I had bought my own home outside Dublin, and met a four-legged angel, in the form of my dog, Jefra, who from the very beginning brought me much love, faithfulness and comfort. I left my job in Dublin and worked at the Glencree Centre for Reconciliation where I made many new and lasting friends. Sylvia, a dear angel in disguise, was one of them. She taught me to look beyond myself and to see and appreciate the world of nature. She literally took me by the hand, brought me to flowers, bent down with me and had me observe the formation, vulnerability, beauty, scent and strength of them. She taught me much about the healing value of music and became very much a positive role model in my life. She, like so many of my other friends, taught me by example the value of open and honest friendship. For that and the full support they have given me over the years, I dearly love and treasure them.

Because I had benefited so much from counselling, I decided to enrol on a two-year course as a trainee counsellor. Life in general was getting better and I had never felt happier and more content. Life was by no means perfect but I was learning such a lot about myself and how I operated in the world that I hoped one day to be able to better the world of others, particularly people who had been raised in care. I continued to be emotionally volatile and quite argumentative, and still had some difficulties accepting the reality that it was not my place to try to control everyone and everything around me. I did however manage to do the required study with ease, but I left the course over what, at the time, I thought was a matter of principle. Essentially what this amounted to was that I couldn't accept a democratic decision made by the remainder of the group. In my attempts to ensure that my right to protest was allowed and respected, I didn't know where to set the boundaries on matters such as this. In the end, I left the course, in protest about something that nowadays would seem to me a relatively minor matter. It perhaps goes without saying that had I been in better control of myself and my emotions, I would have made a wiser decision to complete the course.

In the light of these events, I decided to go to America to make yet another attempt at starting a new life. Family and friends held a party and it was a huge emotional experience, because people were clearly upset about my leaving. One of the most difficult leavings concerned the 'abandonment' of my loyal and beautiful dog Jefra. I cried bitterly about it and felt like a bad abandoning mother. Study, however, continued to hold my interest, and since I was fascinated by the world of counselling, I intended to apply to an American university to do a degree. All went well until the question of funding arose, and then I had to abandon my goals through lack of finance. I stayed with friends and money ran out very quickly. On moving to San Francisco in search of better opportunities, I fast ran out of money and it was there that I came close to cracking from the strain of trying to survive. In desperation, I made a reverse charge call to my good friend Sylvia, who helped guide me through the next steps. Eventually, I made contacts through the Irish Centre and an Irish businessman loaned me a flat, free of charge, to help me on my way. I got a job, made friends with Sharon, my saviour in the US, and stayed with her for several months.

While in America, I got the opportunity to attend many conferences with leading figures in the world of counselling and therapy. Eventually, I was satisfied that I had achieved as much as I could and returned to Ireland, to the people I loved and my dear four-legged angel, Jefra. She eagerly welcomed me back into her life as indeed did my many loyal and great friends.

Though I was now even more convinced that counselling was the career I wanted to pursue, I was undecided about what to do next. Academic qualifications in the world of counselling were being feverishly discussed. As a result I enrolled at the University of East London since it offered a unique course that was not available in Ireland. Although vacillating about whether or not I should emigrate, I planned the move to London. I struggled again over what to do about Jefra and decided to leave her with relatives while I found a suitable home for both of us in London. I thought it was ironic that the major reason I had decided not to get married and have children of my own, was that I swore I would never risk having to abandon those I loved to the care of others. While my dog was not a person, she ranked amongst my dearest and best friends. And here I was, abandoning her again!

Just days before my planned departure my step-father died. Because I hadn't yet made a firm decision to leave and feared my mother's reaction, I hadn't told her of my intentions. I learned of the death of my step-father through a phone call from my step-brother. I was upset, first for myself but mostly for my mother and his family. Thinking now about his funeral it was without doubt the most surreal experience of my life. In the packed church, his family and my mother, the chief mourners, took the front pews. Because my brothers and I were secrets to his relatives and friends, we took seats near the back of the church. For the second time, we found ourselves the 'secret children' at the funeral of a 'secret father'.

To our horror, we saw several friends in the church, and a number of people from my brothers' places of employment. What were we to do? Nearly breathless with anxiety and fear, we struggled to find an explanation for our dilemma. Armed with the words that our family situation was a bit complicated, and that we hoped they would understand if we gave them an explanation at a more convenient time, we faced our kind supporters.

Equally my step-family seemed perplexed and confused when my brothers and I received condolences from our own relatives who didn't know that we were a secret in the step-family. To further confuse matters, my friends and the people from my brothers' places of work offered their condolences to my mother's step-children. Naturally, they had no idea who they were.

My brothers and I attended the interment in Glasnevin cemetery. Standing around the grave, my mother's devastated look haunted me, as I felt powerless in the secretive circumstances to comfort her or even talk to her. I simply could not behave like a dutiful daughter.

The strain was exacerbated when my mother invited us back to her home. We duly sat with her step-children who were probably wondering what we were doing there. Seated opposite my mother, who was overcome with grief, I felt extremely anxious about what I should do. A constant stream of visitors came and went. My mother introduced us by our Christian names, the people dutifully shook our hands but thankfully none of them enquired who we were in relation to our step-father. I felt like a gate-crasher at a function I had no right to attend. As soon as seemed decent, we took our leave and fled the scene of this extremely distressing day.

The whole situation brought home to me, on a very practical level, the implications of living with this monumental secret and lie. I was convinced that it was time to remove myself from the source of many of the emotional issues which emanated from the fact that I colluded with these secrets and lies. It was obvious that I needed some time, space and distance to reflect on the situation, because I determined I would not allow myself to be put in that position again.

Difficult as the circumstances were, I told my mother I was leaving within days for England. With a heavy heart I left the people I loved and Jefra, my dog. Though I was conscious that I was running away from all that was difficult and stifling in Ireland, I also felt, as if guided by an angel, that it was something I had to do if I was to grow to my full potential.

I moved to a tiny student flat provided by the university and settled into college life. Those I loved I missed terribly, so much so that at the end of the first term, my tutor advised me to seriously re-consider whether or not I should return to England after the holiday. I managed just before leaving London to find a new home for myself and Jefra and that went a long way towards affirming my decision to see my study plans through. Towards the end of my first term I realised too that I needed emotional support to help me through the very particular difficulties that arose in my new circumstances.

I sought counselling regarding my childhood in Goldenbridge as I was concerned that dreams and nightmares about it were getting in the way of my studies. In the course of counselling, I learned that my thinking about this was affecting my better judgement and resulted in my behaving in ways that brought about the very situations in my life that I was trying to avoid.

My new counsellor taught me to stand back and observe myself before speaking and acting on impulse. Specifically, she gave me the strategy of holding back by learning to stop and think, to keep a diary of these and bring them to the sessions so that we could explore possible actions and responses to what I considered was disrespectful or aggressive behaviour on the part of others. We then worked with the volatile feelings and emotions which I observed. I became considerably less frazzled and angry and became more objective and balanced in my thinking and behaviour. I also learned that I was not the centre of everybody's universe and that not everybody was out to hurt, upset or humiliate me.

Such strategies for dealing with patterns of behaviour that up to then I had no control over, went a long way towards giving me more control over my life. Because I learned that I didn't need to be so defensive and over-protective of myself, I could instead take the time to reflect and consider my responses. So instead of feeling controlled and bullied, I took charge of myself, and in doing so, took responsibility for my own actions. In this way, my pride and dignity were to some extent restored and I learned that I deserved no less and no more respect than others.

Given that I had been raised in an environment that stripped me of my self-respect and dignity, it was a wonderful experience to move beyond merely knowing in my head that everyone deserved respect. I learned that people, regardless of my judgements and intolerance of them, deserved that which I had for so long desperately wanted and needed for myself. In these ways my aggression, my anger and my tendency to criticise and reject others diminished considerably. Because I didn't need to feel so scared and threatened by others, I began to feel safe, much more secure and confident in this and other areas of my life.

I had experienced severe difficulties with regard to over-dependency on previous counsellors, so I was extremely wary of becoming too involved with my new counsellor. We explored this at length and I found to my great relief that she understood the reasons why this had happened in the past. She warned me of my tendency to cross boundaries and, being mindful of this, she managed to maintain her boundaries without in the least making me feel rejected or unimportant in her life. It helped too that, because I didn't want to repeat old patterns with counsellors, I was highly motivated to co-operate and learn to accept her boundaries as well as discover and learn to respect my own and other people's need for privacy.

My relationship with my mother was an area that we gave much attention to in our sessions. It emerged that many of the problems I had with previous counsellors were largely the result of struggles I had with my mother's non-acceptance of me. I had been particularly affected by my mother's refusal to allow me my identity as her daughter in an acknowledged and open manner. My counsellor supported me through coming to terms with the reality that my mother was unlikely ever to fulfil my emotional needs in these ways. In doing so she allowed me the space to grieve the loss and safely took me to the place where I could accept it without continuing to feel diminished, rejected or abandoned. It was a case of accepting that my mother's rejection of us was her decision and did not necessarily reflect adversely on my brothers or myself, as individuals. Rather it was a reflection of my mother's own inability to cope with and deal honestly with the pressures in her own life. Understanding this gave me the freedom to let go of baggage that ultimately was not mine, and allowed me to return it back to where it firmly belonged, with my mother and others who had hurt and rejected me. The responsibility for the decisions that these people made was suddenly no longer mine and this facilitated me to accept that position. All I had to do now was to learn to accept that I was a lovable and deserving person in my own right and that I needed to take responsibility for loving myself and others. In venturing to do so my perceptions regarding myself, others and the world changed for the better, as did my behaviour. Eventually, I began to feel truly liberated from the people who had imprisoned me in the physical and emotional hells I had known.

Perhaps because I was out of the country where all of my troubles began, I felt as if I had stepped out of a quagmire and could see things more clearly and objectively. It helped that I had anonymity to explore my many problems in a very warm, secure and private space. This may have been helped by the fact that my counsellor had few pre-conceived ideas about Irish society in general. She had a very calm and peaceful demeanour which helped me a lot. I had learned a great deal from my previous experience with counsellors and was motivated and more willing to take responsibility for myself. Whatever it was, I certainly felt that my healing accelerated.

As a result of all that I had learned and effectively put into practice, my self-esteem and confidence rose to new heights. This contributed in very significant ways to my ability and confidence to communicate with my tutors more effectively and honestly. Their status as authority figures was considerably reduced in my eyes and I met them on terms that allowed me be their equal. As a result my intuition that education was my ticket to freedom was validated. In retrospect, I see that this wasn't confined to academic education but encompassed the more personal sphere of self-education that in the end was the most important part of education in the school of life.

Perhaps because my healing accelerated I went through a long and difficult stage of dreams and nightmares in which the demons of my past – frightening nuns, men and women – played increasingly menacing roles. My counsellor was particularly gifted in helping me to analyse these dreams and in time I managed successfully to exorcise most of the ghosts of Goldenbridge which for many years had undermined my recovery.

Having acknowledged the very positive role that counsellors played in my recovery process, I want also to acknowledge that this was augmented by alternative or complementary therapies. Because I had suffered bad health for much of my adult life, I sought the help of qualified and gifted healers, some of whom contributed significantly to enhancing my physical, emotional and spiritual well-being. I learned through their wisdom to take responsibility for what I put into my body and in doing so improved my diet. Through them I learned that I could enhance the quality of the life I now so desperately cherished and wanted to live and enjoy to the full.

Spiritual healing also played an extremely important part in my recovery. Through it I learned the value of all of my life, the past, the present and the future. I had earlier come to the conclusion that emotional needs which had not in the past been met, couldn't retrospectively be met. Through spiritual healing I learned that this was not the case. In the company of my good friends and healers, Bill and Celia, I had the privilege and almost indescribable experience of feeling loved, as if in retrospect. Much of the pain of my past slipped away with that truly healing experience for which I will be forever grateful.

Another, even more potent experience followed when one day I attended a workshop in London, faciliated by two Irish healers, Maura Lundberg and Patrick McMahon. In the course of guided imagery, a kind of meditative exercise, I met with what I refer to as my guardian angel. I was enveloped to my very core in a love that was also indescribably beautiful and healing. This feeling remained with me and has probably been the greatest factor in my healing process. And so this is how I, who had for so many years sowed only tears, was able to come to reap the joy of life, and live in the freedom of angels.